SURPRISED BY GOD
IN THE
MIDST OF HELL

Sharon D. McCormick
7/24/11

SURPRISED BY GOD
IN THE
MIDST OF HELL

*A Pastor's Story of Surviving Horrors
in the Church World*

MEREDITH GILES

Aknowledgements
Cover Design: Michelle Merhige
Editor: Lisa West

Please send your comments about this book to us in care of:

Lone Feather Press
PO Box 189
Feura Bush, NY 12067

Or e-mail: magiles1@juno.com

ISBN   978-0-974-7068-1-8

Printed in the United States of America

-Dedication-

One of my favorite heroes is Sir Winston Churchill. It was he who went out on the rooftop during an air raid on London and shook his fists at the enemy as bombs whizzed all around him. When once giving a speech to a military academy, he simply stood and told them, "Never, never quit!" and then went and sat down. Stephen, you are my Winston. You are my hero. Many have been the times you have shaken your fists at the enemy declaring to all of us around you, "We will never, never quit!" Thank you, dear Husband. Our congregation thanks you, and in fact, we would not even be a congregation today if it weren't for the price you have paid. Know that you are dearly loved and treasured as husband, father and pastor, and I believe someday you will hear for yourself from the Lover of your soul, "Well done, thou good and faithful servant."

CONTENTS

FOREWORD

The spiritual strength of our lives and ministries is often shaped and molded by God in extreme times of testing. The result is the ability to touch the life of another in a significant way. Meredith, knows what testing is. She perhaps is one of the most spiritually strong women we know. She would tell you she is, "strong in the Lord and in the power of His Might." Her book is a picture of the strength of God revealed in a person who was reared and discipled in the Pentecostal faith and doctrine. The story she writes hits that faith and doctrine head on. However, thank God the collision is not fatal.

What we take away from this book is the certainty that with God's help we are able to face the most extreme circumstances. When all the forces of hell gather around and Satan comes violently, yet we are able to stand because of the truth we learn from scripture. The surprising grace of God is found in the midst of all situations. You will read a literal battle plan for everyone involved in spiritual ministry. Please do not misunderstand the author. Truth is simply truth. This book is not a vendetta against anyone. If anything, it should leave you with a sense of direction and purpose even in the darkness; it is a guide.

If the Giles Family and this church can just hang in there and trust an unfailing God when they cannot see the battle raging in the spiritual background, it is certain they will break through for the kingdom of God. Most people would throw up their hands in despair and flee the scene.

Yet in the middle of a very sinister plot to destroy this church, all the elements for victory and success are there. It may seem intriguing and fascinating reading now. But as a bystander, we know it was not fun while it was happening.

Watching from a distance, we observe the growth and maturity of a couple dedicated to ministry and to the particular vineyard they have been given: a church that will not die and a people who learn loyalty and commitment. It is a picture of the ongoing struggle of Christ's church as He continues to mature it.

Be a courageous warrior. This book will relentlessly urge you to keep going no matter what, even as tears may blind your eyes. While the "dark night" of your soul seems forever, **KEEP GOING**. How does this saga of survival end for the church?

Well, you will have to read it to find out the answer. We assure you God is on the scene at every turn. He does know how to surprise us.

Drs. David and Jeanne Wyns

FROM THE AUTHOR

In the pages which follow, I hope to show by way of my own experience that the Name of Jesus is enough, sovereign, and always present. There are fellow travelers who have walked along with me on this journey who are dear and precious to me. They too, have experienced the magnificence of our Father, His tender care and all encompassing love for us in such intimate ways. These fellow travelers have shared their lives with me and have blessed me along the way.

To my fellow brothers and sisters in ministry, may these thoughts breathe life and hope to you in the depths of any darkness you may be walking through and shine light and great hope, heart skipping hope, that God is with you, knows all about you and your circumstances and is more than able to make a way where there seems to be no way. May this book be a tool of hope and an anchor in your time of storm.

To all of the body of Christ, may this book become a little manual of thought provoking experiences and discussion, strengthening and enlarging the body to come into a stronger posture to bring change in this ever changing world for good and to wage war against the enemy of our souls, forever to be aware of his sly, evil schemes.

My prayer is that my story will speak to yours.

Psalm 139:1-8

O Lord, You have searched
me (thoroughly) and have known
me. You know my downsitting and
my uprising; You understand my
thought afar off. You sift and search out
my path and my lying down, and You are
acquainted with all my ways. For there is not
a word in my tongue (still unuttered), but, behold, O Lord, You know it altogether. You have
beset me and shut me in behind and before, and
You have laid your hand upon me. Your (infinite) knowledge is too wonderful for me; it is high
above me, I cannot reach it. Where could I go
from Your Spirit? Or where could I flee from
Your presence? If I ascend up into heaven, You
are there; *if I make my bed in hell*, behold, You
are there. If I take the wings of the morning or
dwell in the uttermost parts of the sea, even
there shall Your hand lead me, and Your right
hand shall hold me. If I say, surely the darkness shall cover me and the night shall be
(the only) light about me, even the
darkness hides nothing from You,
but the night shines as the day;
the darkness and the light
are both alike to You.

ONE

~

THE CALL

Have you ever experienced such a vast array of emotions that you felt like you would never be able to express them in such a way that others could fully understand and connect with you? This is how I feel as I begin the telling of this tale. My mind and spirit are full of whirling memories and deep wounds that have healed over, leaving scars. Yet, I believe if I can articulate to you what really happened and what the Lord has taught us while we were on this journey, maybe, just maybe, we can be a source of healing balm and much needed encouragement to someone who, like us, has found themselves on a road never traveled or planned. In my mind, these types of journeys always were traversed by others...not us. Theirs were stories that made for good reading. They were the survivors of such journeys... not us. But, here we are, ready to tell our tale.

And so the telling of my journey begins...the dark night of my soul.

I was born and raised in the beautiful state of Maine. So was my husband. The sense of the "call of God" on my life probably was there as early as five years of age. I jokingly tell people that I was conceived in church. I remember falling asleep under the pews and waking up under the pews and then just falling asleep again under the pews where a little bed had been made for me. My family loved the Lord, and we were always faithful to His house and careful to live by the precepts of His Word.

I grew up "in the house" (the church), and never had seen any serious church problems among the believers. My pastor was a solid, old veteran of the faith. His name was Pastor Crabtree. He had snow white hair, walked like he had a straight stick up his back, and never, ever compromised the Word of God, in the pulpit or out.

My Christian heritage goes back even generationally. My great-grandmother was saved under William Booth, founder of the Salvation Army. In fact, my grandmother has told us that General Booth used to send her dear mother out to preach the Gospel in the villages outside of London. I have read where General Booth stated that his few good men were women. Well, it seems my great gram was one of those. Christianity was in my blood...even from way back when.

I was taught by my godly parents, pastors, and Sunday school teachers that God had a breathtaking plan for my life and if I would fully surrender my all to Him, He would lead, direct and guide me each step of life's way. I grew, finished high school and had to make the decision to go to a secular university to study law or journalism, both of which I had entertained pursuing for years. My high school years had been a long season of great wrestling over this decision of what I would do with my life. Always though, there had been a strong inner pull of the Holy Spirit to follow **His** leading to study for the ministry. Towards the end of my senior year I had gotten past my wrestling with indecision and had finally come to a complete heart surrender to what I knew God was asking of me. I finally paid attention fully to the nudging of the Holy Spirit in my heart and knew what I had to do. The choice was made – I would study for the ministry.

During my last year of high school, this intensely handsome, young man named Stephen, had started coming to my home church. I thought he had the most gorgeous teeth, was built nice, and even dressed attractively. He was just out of the Marine Corp and had given his heart to the Lord. He seemed to be really in love with Him. We began to see each other, and yes, we fell in love. I had never felt this way about anyone before. I wanted to be with him all the time. Stephen had a terrific sense of humor and made me laugh alot. Besides, I thought he was very good looking! I was to learn later that his gorgeous teeth were caps and he had won his fine looking clothes in a battalion poker game while he was serving in the Marines. I guess the joke was on me! God has His ways!

As we started to spend time together, we began to share with each other all our various hopes and dreams. I made it very clear that I knew I had a calling from the Lord to study for the ministry. Stephen was not against this for me, but he seemed to become agitated whenever I would bring up the subject. Unbeknownst to me, he had been feeling the tug of God to go into the ministry, yet he hadn't fully surrendered his will to the Lord. His academic experiences had not always been positive ones and his confidence in the idea of going to college, looked overwhelming, to say the least. He also had been offered some excellent positions as a carpenter, with opportunities that included good growth and future promotion. For me though, I could not ignore the pull of God on my life and I told him so.

Finally, one day Stephen had a divine encounter with God, a Damascus road experience you could say. He completely surrendered his will to the Lord, immediately applied for and was accepted into the college I was going to attend within weeks of its beginning semester.

We were married on a steamy, hot day in July and then in September, we went off to Zion Bible Institute in Providence, Rhode Island with our tiny blue Vega packed to the gills and one hundred dollars in our pocket. We survived this learning experience by living in a small, humble apartment, both of us sleeping on a twin bed and Stephen cleaning up floors and countertops for a bakery down the road and me cleaning houses.

These years of intense training were not as glamorous as we had envisioned, yet God was always faithful to us. Our college days were probably very similar to others who have been trained to become ministers of the Gospel. Hard work and sacrifice, in and of themselves, were heavenly courses, with the Spirit of God as the Instructor.

We then took our first pastorate as rookie pastors in the northernmost city in Maine, Caribou. We were there four years...four long, cold years. The car tires used to stick to the road as the temperatures would dip as low as forty degrees below zero.

As I look back, I can see many of the lessons learned there, were training us for the journey He had prepared for us further along in our lives. The people for the most part, were friendly and warm. Yet there were some who had run from church to church, causing strife and division wherever they happened to land. Some of them were even on the board of our church.

If we did exactly as they wanted, preached the way they enjoyed, and if we allowed ourselves to be tucked right under their arms to control, then we would get our big fat paycheck of seventy five dollars a week. If we preached what God impressed us to preach, we usually ruffled too many feathers, and our big fat paycheck would be put on indefinite hold.

Through it all, God was faithful to us. We never went hungry and God had a multitude of other ways of providing. For example, Stephen's G.I. Bill was a continued blessing as he attended the University of Maine, furthering his education, and was paid to do so.

Our prayer lives had to become stronger as we learned to wrestle with carnal and demonic activity. At the end of the fourth year, we felt the releasing of the Lord to move on to the next phase of our lives.

Our summer of freedom was spent living on a quaint farm nestled in a field off a dirt road, not far from where my family homestead stood. During our summer, we ministered weekends in many different churches from churches down on the coast to works dotted throughout central Maine all the way back to northern Maine. We were happy, but still, we had a sense that the Lord had a specific place for us to be planted. We now had three babies, Andrea, five, Benjamin, three, and our two month old newborn, Heather, who had just arrived before leaving Caribou. We needed to settle into the plan God had for us, whatever was in His heart.

After we graduated from college, we had been accepted as members of a prominent denomination, holding credentials with them. After leaving Caribou, we once again polished our résumé, submitted it to the denominational district office, then we waited and prayed.

Towards the end of the summer we received a call from a place in the state of New York. You must understand that when someone from Maine hears the words "New York," they immediately think of New York City. My family went straight into a holy uproar! They didn't want us going far from home into that jungle of a city. What was wrong with us for even considering it? Yet as we prayed concerning this interesting invitation, we felt the pull of God to at least go and see what it was like. We packed up our car, taking only little Heather with us, and leaving the other two kids with Grandma. We felt like Abraham, not knowing where he was going, only that we were to go.

Our guest church had invited us to be with them over a weekend. As we were traveling, I still felt a little apprehensive, yet with a deep desire to do God's will. We arrived after an eight hour journey and were placed with a warm couple whose names were Frank and Mary. They lived in a beautifully kept home that looked like something right out of a Martha Stewart magazine. They gave up their comfortable bedroom for us and had even arranged a little crib for baby Heather to sleep in. It was perfect for her. We felt at home right away with them. Mary was a great cook and both of them told us some pretty fascinating stories about their lives, especially their experiences during World War II.

The next day was the dreaded interview. I was somewhat nervous. My stomach kept doing those awfully weird flip flops you always get when you don't want to. Stephen seemed to be putting his best foot forward. For me, the more I saw of the place, the less I honestly liked it. It was a totally different atmosphere than what I was used to. Everyone seemed to project this strict attitude of "this is the way things are done around here and God help you if you don't do them that way." This was not how I had been raised. Where we came from, everyone was comfortable with each other, personable and friendly. Oh yes, people here were nice enough and seemed excited about us being there, yet it wasn't the same. "Oh, Lord," I quietly and fervently prayed, "What **are** You doing?"

We had dinner at another family's home, the Browns, that evening, and then came the ominous Sunday. We both dressed to look our best, Stephen in a crisp, freshly pressed white shirt with his newly dry-cleaned dark blue suit free of lint, and me in a neat, hopefully not too bold dress, trying to look put together without seeming to be too flashy.

We prayed earnestly that we would know the mind of Christ concerning the relationship of this church with us.

When we arrived at the church building, we were met by a delegated board member, Joe, who seemed really hungry for a genuine move of God. He chatted with us for awhile and as we talked, generally informed us that the congregation was used to a much shorter service than we were. Yet he encouraged us to allow God to move as we felt He was leading us. Of course, this kind of announcement served only to set us on edge. Joe continued to familiarize us with the facility by walking us through all the small classrooms for the various ministries including their private day school, grades kindergarten through twelth.

The congregation was thrilled that I happened to be an accomplished pianist and worship leader. This seemed to raise the enthusiasm of everyone to a higher pitch than I had seen in the stuffy private board meeting. Of course, my husband preached a stirring message, explaining to them what he would expect if he came to be their pastor. I didn't think they would think much of that. It seemed like a very conservative group and change may not have been the thing they were really looking for. You see, they had told us that they had already gone through at least ten, if not more candidates for pastor. As I saw it, Stephen's forthrightness would be a little too much for them.

"Phew," I thought. "We won't have to come here!" Yet even as he spoke, people were responding as if receiving a drink of cold water after a long time in a dry, dusty desert.

"Oh, no," I thought. "Lord, You really wouldn't make us come to **this** place!" I clutched Heather nestled in my arms asleep, closer to my bosom and tried to conjure up memories of home sweet home and warm services where I had enjoyed the awesome Presence of God without having to war over anything or anyone.

The service ended. Frank and Mary took us home for a delicious Sunday dinner and a well deserved nap. I was alone with Heather in the upstairs bedroom, so I closed my eyes and began to talk this very strange situation over with God. "Father, you know we don't really fit in here well at all. This isn't what we are used to." I believe there must have been a little whine in my voice as I began to pray. Absolute silence on God's part. I continued to pray for awhile, venting all my emotions as only I can do.

Then I came up with this wonderful idea. "Lord, I'll willingly come here only if You make the congregational vote tonight one hundred percent. Then I will know this is where You want us." I thought I really had the Lord then. It was unheard of for someone candidating, especially after so many others had not been received as their pastor, for us then to receive a unanimous vote. "Ha, ha," I thought. "No way were we coming back here to this dead place!"

After our Sunday meal, and a nice, long snooze, we journeyed back to the church for the evening service and then the final vote. I would be glad to be heading back home. I thought to myself this all was a pretty much done deal, open and shut after my afternoon talk with God. Stephen, of course, preached another powerfully anointed message that ministered life to people.

Then we were asked to step outside, away from where the congregation was going to hold their meeting, to wait while the business at hand was taken care of. I remember snuggling Heather in my arms while talking to one of the teachers of the private school that was part of the ministry of the church. He wasn't an official member and didn't need to be involved in the voting process. Tim didn't know whether to encourage us that we would be coming there to pastor or to try to prepare us for a negative response. He himself had had his extreme highs and lows working in the school and with these people. I knew I just wanted to be out of there (the sooner the better), and to be on our way home. Yet the words of my prayer seemed to be echoing hauntingly in my mind. I earnestly tried to push that Voice out. Yes, I had prayed one hundred percent, but it would be impossible! It was unheard of!

We paced outside in the church driveway with our new friend, Tim for about twenty minutes. Then loud cheer-

~

YES, I HAD PRAYED ONE HUNDRED
PERCENT, BUT IT WOULD BE IMPOSSIBLE!
IT WAS UNHEARD OF!

~

ing was heard coming from the inside. As I turned to look through the elevated windows at what was happening, I saw everyone standing to their feet and praising the Lord with clapping and shouts of joy. "Oh, no," I thought wistfully, "They either love us or they truly hate us!"

One of the ushers on duty came out quickly and asked us to come back in. We then were led down the middle aisle and escorted to the front pew. Deacon, the leader of the pack, was presiding over the voting meeting and he continued to chair after we were seated. He looked directly at my husband with a big smile on his face and said, "Well, Pastor." Stephen being called Pastor was not a good sign for me! I could feel perspiration break out down the center of my back. "We would like to have you come and lead us. We have been waiting for a long time for the right man and we believe you are the one. Oh, yes, and by the way…the vote was one hundred percent, the first time in the history of this church!" "Good Lord, NO!!" I could hear myself screaming within myself.

My heart sank to the absolute bottom of my feet! I hadn't even shared my outrageous fleece with my husband. All along he had seemed much more open to the idea of coming here than me. Stephen stood and slowly responded that he would like some time to pray about it. They all consented, but asked that we not take too long as they were very anxious for us to begin our ministry among them.

The long ride home up I-95 to Maine was one of tumultuous discussion, sometimes loud, sometimes quiet and introspective, yet with a great sense of the hovering of the Lord over our lives. When I finally shared the drastic prayer I had prayed that Sunday afternoon with Stephen, he got extremely quiet. It seemed that the Lord had been dealing strongly with him, too, even before I had said anything.

~

THE LONG RIDE HOME UP I-95 TO MAINE WAS ONE OF TUMULTUOUS DISCUSSION, SOMETIMES LOUD, SOMETIMES QUIET AND INTROSPECTIVE, YET WITH A GREAT SENSE OF THE HOVERING OF THE LORD OVER OUR LIVES.

~

We arrived home to our little farmhouse and children, already knowing what God was saying. In a few short weeks we were to go to New York and begin to pastor these people.

With tearful farewells, much double checking of phone numbers, with many plans to write and call, we were on our way.

"Now the Lord said to Abram, 'Go for yourself away from your own country, from your relatives and your father's house, to the land that I will show you.' So Abram departed, as the Lord had directed him." And so, just as it was with Abram, so it was with us.

~ PERSONAL REFLECTIONS ~

The Divine does not work separately from the human, but with it and by it. "Now the Lord God had said unto Abraham, get thee out of thy country." The "Divine call" is no less Divine in our lives as it was in Abraham's; it may be totally dissimilar in a different age and varied setting, but nonetheless still "Divine." The summons in one's life is from the Lord. It may come in a myriad of different forms. It, many times, as with Abraham, will be explicit. He was to leave all. It was an unambiguous summons, and it was repeated.

These kinds of calls are usually opposed to our carnal inclinations. Dangers await those who should respond to the call, for "the Canaanite was then in the land." Fortunate for those starting out, they are unawares of the enemy waiting in inconspicuous nooks and crannies of unsuspecting turns and various crossroads along their way. If all truth was to be known ahead of time, many would never start out in following the "Voice of the Divine."

Abraham had a promise that was sufficient enough for the time. God does not reveal all the riches of His grace at once. Abraham went forth in obedience from the plain of Chaldea to the land which God had spoken to him of, ever listening to the "Voice" that only Abraham could hear.

The measure of our faith is the measure of the blessing we shall convey to others. We sometimes hinder the operation of God's promise by our self-righteous humility, which ignores the fact that God often uses the "weak

~

THERE MUST BE FAITH IN GOD'S
CONTINUING WORKING. HE CAN MAKE
THE FUTURE FRUITFUL
IN PROPORTION TO OUR FAITH.

~

things of the world to confound the things that are mighty." There must be faith in God's continuing working. He can make the future fruitful in proportion to our faith. Look at what he made of Paul, Luther, Wigglesworth, Wesley, Moody and Whitfield because they were all men of strong faith.

Probably Abraham never gave much thought of the honor which would come to him; but God adapted His promise to that which He knew to be the desire of the secret soul of Abraham. Seeing a longing in the heart to lift men to a higher level, he gratifies it by making Abraham a blessing. All should cherish such desires. To live an aimless life is a disgrace and sin, but to live to bless others is Divine.

THOUGHTS TO PONDER

♦ Why does the "Divine" not work separately but rather randomly of human beings?

♦ Why is the "call of God" usually opposed to carnal inclinations?

♦ The measure of our faith is the measure of the blessing we shall convey to others. He can make the future fruitful in proportion to our faith. Is this concept actively working through your life?

♦ God adapted His promise to that which He knew to be the desire of the secret soul of Abraham. What secret desires has God planned and seen in your heart? Are you moving forward in quick obedience to His "Voice" concerning these secret things?

TWO

~

AGGRESSIVE YIELDEDNESS

We arrived to begin our little pastorate late in the fall of 1981. Baby Heather was now three months old. Our other two children, Andrea and Benjamin, were a rambunctious five and three years of age. This was an enormous step for us, yet we felt the guiding Hand of the Lord upon us.

The parsonage was in good shape. We had a spacious living room, a comfortable dining room and an efficient kitchen with extra counter space. Each family member would have their own bedroom. A huge back yard only added to our excitement as the kids envisioned lots of playtime there. I felt blessed moving into this attractive home, yet I was still pining a little with homesickness for our snug farmhouse and open beautiful countryside in far away Maine.

I remember the day we were moving our furniture into the parsonage. There was a small group of men from the church who had arrived to help us unload our things. One gnarly looking man in particular, showed up to help. He was a little different to say the least. His name was David. His long hair went all the way down his back. He seemed kindly enough but he looked a bit scary. I quietly pulled Stephen to one side of the garage and whispered softly in his ear, "You'd better watch out for that one. He may try to steal something."

As the days went on, David would stop by quite often and look in on us. He had never been in church and had never accepted the Lord. As their friendship grew, Stephen and David began sitting up all hours of the night. Stephen would answer David's many questions about God and His Word. Then one day he started attending services. After what seemed to be an eternity of soul searching and many questions asked and answered, David finally surrendered his life to Jesus. This was the beginning of my husband winning many men to the Lord. His outrageous sense of humor and homespun ways seemed to make others feel very comfortable and they could easily relate and open up with him.

David, his gentle wife, Stacey and their children eventually all came to know the Lord. He and his family have been very dear and precious friends to us and our children ever since.

We made many new friends and God visited the services in a powerful way. I felt a strong desire to work with the youth. I began some services and activities just for them. We started with just three, but soon grew to as high as seventy-five young people in attendance. As I look back now, I realize that we were having a sovereign move of God in those days. Young people were traveling, some of them thirty and forty miles to be in the services. They were coming from broken, dysfunctional homes, really needy and hurting. Some were bleeding all over emotionally and didn't have anywhere else to turn. God met them in that little country church. At one time we had as many as twenty-five attending Bible college. Many of them, to this day, are in full or part-time ministry doing a powerful work for the Lord.

In God's plan, there were to be two more priceless gifts given to the Giles family during those years. Blonde haired and blue eyed Judah was born in 1985, and Jordan, with blonde hair and big blueberry eyes was born in 1987. I call them my double portion. All five of our children have truly been a great blessing and joy to us.

The Giles kids were all enrolled in the church academy. It was a wonderful school with good curriculum and lots of other fun children to grow up with and enjoy. Of course, it had its challenges, but overall, the school was a blessing to many families throughout the years.

The church was growing to full capacity. The tiny sanctuary was almost packed every service and the small classrooms downstairs were tightly overcrowded. After having been their pastors for nine years, we were bursting at the seams. We began to pray and seek God for His direction. By now, numerous parents from the influx of youth were coming in because they had seen the changes in their young person and came to the church searching to find out what their changed children had found. These inquisitive parents were giving their lives to the Lord and beginning to grow in awesome ways. Everyone was excited to be a part of what God was doing.

Stephen, for some reason unknown to me, suddenly became greatly agitated and irritable. He became snappy at everyone around him. Wisely I kept my distance, walked softly around him and prayed asking God to sort out whatever was going on inside of him.

One night I couldn't get this passage of Scripture out of my mind. I knew I had to go to him in the dimly lit bedroom where he was shut in alone and read this particular passage to him. I believe now it was something concerning obedience. I remember fervently praying before I entered his "cave of seclusion," asking the Lord to help me not to get upset if he got heated with me.

I quietly went in and sat down nervously beside him on the bed. I told him I had a scripture for him. As I began to gently read, he began to sob like a baby. Something was breaking in him. God had been dealing with him to go away on a two week fast. It seemed God was drawing him aside to speak to him. Stephen had not wanted to, not just because God was asking him to fast, but because God had been dealing with him about getting alone with Him to listen to what He wanted to say concerning building a new facility to accommodate his growing congregation. He had been wrestling with this thought because he felt very content and fulfilled the way things were. We were financially comfortable and growing as a church and everyone was on board to help with this growth in whatever way they could. Now here he was, being confronted by God to draw away and listen, yes, really listen to something more God wanted to speak to him.

Stephen is one who may take a long time to make up his mind, but once he has made a decision, he will move forward with it in a bulldog fashion. Being a former Marine, he can bring himself to great measures of discipline when called upon.

Once the decision was finalized that he would go on this fast, a few phone calls were made to make the ar-

~

THEY HAD A HEART THAT SAW THE HARVEST FIELDS ALL AROUND THEM AND TRULY WANTED TO BE EFFECTIVE LABORERS IN THOSE FIELDS.

~

rangements. Deacon came by and picked him up to drive Stephen to a motel in the city. Stephen later called with his room and phone number and a plan was made that we would only talk to each other once every night during the fast. We both were to seek the Lord for His direction. I would do a partial fast, eating only a bowl of soup once a day as I had to oversee everything, family and church, while he was away.

Beth, a committed young lady in our youth group, and her newly saved uncle, Will, (David's oldest son), were to come and stay with me to help with the children, run errands, mainly just to be a support during this season of prayer.

The people were told about the fast and they, too, began to seek the Lord earnestly with us. These eager people were hungry for whatever God wanted to do. They had a heart that saw the harvest fields all around them and truly wanted to be effective laborers in those fields.

Stephen and I would share with each other every night by phone. During the day, I would shut myself away in prayer in my little office as much as possible, writing down Scripture and any leading I received in prayer. Stephen would do the same. We would share with each other the things God was speaking to us every day. It was amazing how the Holy Spirit was revealing similar things to us both as we waited on Him. This gave us a great confidence that He was the One leading us.

Stephen came back home only on Sunday mornings during the fourteen days. He looked so thin and pale. He literally had to hang on to the sides of the pulpit as he sincerely shared from his heart what the Lord was impressing on him during the fast.

Within the last week of the fast, Stephen felt, as a church, we needed to make a prayer caravan around a circumference of the communities within a twenty mile radius of our church. We were to earnestly pray as we went together, a prayer of agreement, in groups in the cars and vans, and break sticks over each community, believing God to do a powerful work in each one. We then were to bring the sticks back to the church and burn them symbolizing the breaking of Satan's power over the area.

Many arrived early that morning, lining the altar of the church kneeling in prayer before starting the caravan. It was a moving time as we all had drawn closer to the Lord as we had waited on Him in the past few weeks and were progressing by active faith to believe Him for a tremendous harvest of souls.

During the fourteen days of fasting and prayer, the Lord impressed Stephen to check into a certain piece of property near the city on a very prominent highway which happened to be a main artery into the city. He told one of the main board members, Deacon, about it and asked if he were familiar with it. Deacon about fell off his chair! A man had been in his office several times over the last two weeks trying to pointedly entice him to purchase this very piece of land. Deacon himself was not interested, but now upon hearing this news from his pastor, felt he should talk to the man again right away.

You see, Deacon, who had served on the church board for many years, was an influential businessman, a multi-millionaire to be exact. He always had a good eye for profitable land at good prices. He began to investigate this property more with an ear tuned to buying it. There were some questions about a little radio station being part of the land for sale. He discussed this with Pastor who was still on the fast and Pastor told him the radio station was part of the property as he had been shown by the Lord. Sure enough, when he went back to check the map again with the seller, the old radio station was part of the property.

Stephen came home and shared with the church board and then later the people, the piece of property the Lord had shown him we were to build on. Everyone was so excited, yet all were asked to pray and seek God for further confirmation. Stephen felt it was really important that no one feel left out or left behind. In fact, he felt the Lord had stirred him that everyone was to be a part of the move, that God had a great master plan He was performing.

The plan was presented slowly to the congregation, questions answered along the way. The plan included how to finance the land and the building of a new church without having to go into a great amount of debt. As pastor, my husband had a true shepherd's heart in wanting to see that everyone, including the older sheep that had been in our present facility for many years, were comfortable with this move.

It came time for the vote as to whether the congregation felt it was God or not to buy this piece of land and build a new facility. What a night! The vote was taken and it came back in favor of going forward.

Deacon went within a few days and purchased all twenty acres that Pastor had seen while waiting on the Lord. The price per acre at that time was ten thousand dollars an acre. Later the value of the land would increase to three hundred thousand dollars or more per acre. Most of this land would be designated to be used for building and Deacon would keep several acres to resell later. Oh, how we can trust the timing of the Lord!

Research was done as to what type of building to build and the financial plan was put in place. A budget had been set at eight hundred thousand dollars: two hundred thousand could likely be raised from pledges; two hundred thousand from the sale of another piece of property the church owned near the old facility; two hundred thousand from the sale of the old church; and we then would carry a two hundred thousand dollar mortgage. Preparations began and the ground breaking took place in November of 1988. The footings were set and the superstructure was erected in March of 1989.

One particular service stays fresh in my mind, where the Spirit of the Lord led us to designate from among the men of the congregation, two wonderful men whom God had sovereignly brought to be a part of our work. They were gifted builders. Exodus 36:1 says, "Bezalel and Aholiab and every wisehearted man in whom the Lord has put wisdom and understanding to know how to do all the work for the service of the sanctuary shall work according to all that the Lord has commanded." The Lord had the congregation during the service, tie workmen's carpenter aprons around each of them. God was telling them, even as men of old had been chosen to do the work of building special temples for the Lord, so these two talented men were to oversee the building of the new church. The Presence of the Lord was truly powerful that day! We all wiped tears from our eyes and rejoiced together over how God was leading.

One of these men, Carl, along with his wife, Loraine, felt that the Lord wanted them to sell their home and give fifty thousand dollars towards the building project. A sacrificial offering day was set aside. Everyone from the youngest to the oldest was asked to pray and see what God would have each to give. Many people gave large amounts of money as led by the Lord to this project. It wasn't just one or two. It was everyone giving from the poorest to the wealthiest, the youngest to the oldest. People were enthused and full of great joy and expectation wanting to help in whatever way they could.

Deacon was involved in a big business deal he felt was going to bring a great profit. At the time of the sacrificial offering, he came forward, stood at the altar, and wept before God. God had been doing a deep work in his life. I believe he had a calling from the Lord to set himself aside for more ministry than what he presently was doing. Deacon had spoken much about brokenness and had been seeking the Lord to do this powerful work in his own heart. He wept openly committing to pledge 80% of the profits from this particular deal back into the church and other ministry here and abroad. Deacon was gifted in many areas of his life and I believe he sensed the call of God intensely to surrender his all to the Lord and allow God to use him mightily to affect the world around him and fields afar. What tremendous opportunity and challenge lay before him. Only God knew what He had purposed in His heart for Deacon.

One day during this time period, I had just laid the kids down for an afternoon nap, and as was my usual habit, I went into the living room to pray. This was a time I looked forward to everyday where I would have very few interruptions. As I was praying, I saw in my "mind's eye," (not unlike what Peter experienced in Acts 10 while on the rooftop praying), a very wealthy man from my home town area in Maine. He was a well known businessman. He was standing in his gun shop, looking at his cash register. He seemed to be intent on counting his money.

Then a sad look would come over his face and he would look out the big window in the front of his store. The sense in my spirit was that he knew there were people out there hurting and if he chose, he could help them, yet he would look back at his cash register with great zeal and enthusiasm. And then fleetingly he would look out the window again, only to turn back to his cash register.

The picture in my mind's eye then grew small and moved to a corner of my vision. Up came another picture. It was almost like being in a movie theater. I saw next what appeared to be a big open room in an old barn. Hay was strewn everywhere. I could almost smell the pungent odors of stalled animals. As I overlooked this room, in walked a very old woman, with a weathered, wrinkly face. She wore a kerchief on her head, tied under her chin. She knelt painfully in the hay and began to pray quietly with tears streaming from her eyes, with a strained expression on her face, beseeching God to help. She was in great distress.

Soon a younger man walked in wearing a flat hat, a wool suit jacket, with his shirt underneath, buttoned up to his neck. He appeared to be her son. He too knelt down in the hay beside the old woman. He began to pray just as earnestly as she was. They appeared to be extremely desperate and in some kind of immediate danger.

I began to cry out to God for them, as my heart began to feel the burden of their prayers. I cried out to the Lord to help me understand what I was seeing.

The vision would go from one picture of the businessman in his shop, back to the two people praying in the barn. I asked the Lord, "What are they asking you for? What kind of danger are they in? Who are they?" At first I thought they were homeless people. Yet that didn't seem to feel right. Then the Lord spoke into my heart that these were people in the then Soviet Union who were in grave danger. They were asking God to stir someone in America to help them get out of their own country.

God then showed me the selfish businessman again and how He had tried to deal with his cold, hard heart, yet he was too wrapped up in making money to listen to the Voice of God. The picture would switch back to the two in prayer. My spirit became very heavy for these people. The vision would not leave me.

I shared it with my husband who began to seek the Lord as to why God had shown this to me. We also felt that I was to share this vision with the church congregation. People began to pray for revelation to come.

Stephen, a while later, had a dream from the Lord. In the dream he was in his old, red pickup truck. He was driving steadily along, when all of a sudden, his truck started going backwards. He had no control over it. As it backed up, it went around something in the road. Before him, on the road in the dream, was a wooly blanket. As he looked at it wondering what it was doing there, the blanket began to move and then turned into sheep. The sheep all got up and ran ahead of his truck. The truck started to go forward giving plenty of space for the sheep to walk on ahead. The sheep went on their way under the guidance and protection of the truck. Then they went around a bend and were gone. End of dream.

Now we were really wondering what the Lord was trying to say. We carried my vision and this dream in us for about ten months, praying over them and listening.

One day we were at a meeting where a man from the Soviet Union was begging churches to sponsor Soviet Christians whose very lives were in danger. Sponsors were needed or they had no future other than more persecution and the threat of prison. Our hearts leaped within both of us! This was it! God wanted us to become a sponsor and help these people! But, we were in the middle of a building project! After much prayer, it was certain that the Lord was saying to us as a congregation and pastors, that He was requiring this sacrifice of love for these people and for us not to be too wrapped up in ourselves for us to stop and help them. We felt just as Stephen's red pickup went backwards, we had to slow down and back up and help these dear precious people, sheep of God's pasture, get to a safe haven of refuge.

~

THERE WERE MANY TEARS OVER THESE PEOPLE IN PRAYER AND IT WAS AGREED UPON THAT THE LORD WAS LEADING US TO DO JUST WHAT WE HAD FELT IN THE VISION AND DREAM...HELP.

~

We went home and shared it with the people of our congregation. There were many tears over these people in prayer and it was agreed upon that the Lord was leading us to do just what we had felt in the vision and dream...help.

2 Corinthians 9:9 says, "As it is written, he (the benevolent person) scatters abroad; He gives to the poor; His deeds of justice and goodness and kindness and benevolence will go on and endure forever!"

We applied to be sponsors and agreed to sponsor two families: the Budinskis and the Kolodychuks, fifteen members in all between the two families. Apartments were rented and furnished. Money was raised for food and supplies and a few translators were found.

The day came for them to arrive. Everyone from the church wanted to be there to greet them at the airport. Several of the news stations caught wind of it and showed up to greet them, too. This was big stuff for our small church!

Finally the plane arrived! Everyone was clapping as we pressed our noses against the big airport windows! Then finally the doors from the runways opened and the first one we were to see walking in was an old woman named Maria, with a weathered, wrinkly face wearing an old coat and a kerchief on her head tied under her chin. Everyone gasped! This was the old woman seen in the day vision!

Next entered a younger man wearing a flat hat with a wool jacket, with his shirt underneath buttoned up to his neck! Her son! Another gasp! He was the very one seen in the dream!

Next to arrive were the rest of the family members looking tired, worn and hungry. Our hearts went out to them. What a drastic step to take to have religious freedom. I was reminded of 2 Corinthians 4:8,9 which says, "We are pursued (persecuted and hard driven), but not deserted (to stand alone); we are struck down to the ground, but never struck out and destroyed; Always carrying about in the body the liability and exposure to the same putting to death that the Lord Jesus suffered, so that the resurrection life of Jesus also may be shown forth by and in our bodies." Oh, how much Jesus must have meant to them!

A local news reporter, through a translator, stopped the old woman, Maria and asked her, "Why did you want to come to America?" She straightforwardly answered him through the translator, "Because when I want to worship God openly and freely pray and honor Him, I am grabbed by the neck and thrown to the ground!" She waved her arms in harsh demonstration to show him. I could see a wet tear begin to slide down the reporter's face. He quietly replied to this dear old woman, "Welcome to America."

~ PERSONAL REFLECTIONS ~

There are specific times within your ministry when your prayers may not be answered as quickly as you may want them to be. There are certain distinctive situations when our prayers aren't answered because Father God is working out other dynamics of importance in the body of Christ. Many times we will not be able to see these dynamics with our human eyes; then at other times, He will give us glimpses into His master plan. The Lord expects us only to believe, nothing else. True faith doesn't have a plan B standing in the wings ready in case the way of our faith fails. Faith is scripted to do only one thing: it is to only believe.

It is extremely easy to become hyper-focused on your given vision. It is extremely easy to overly internalize, seeing only **your** work and desiring to hear what God has to speak to **you**. Sudden changes on the journey and delayed answers in search of God's heart, test our truly hearing God's Voice and then being obedient to move at His direction or to stand still at His word. When we are hyper-focused on raising funds for our vision, and then God speaks and requires a sacrifice along the way for someone else—

this really is a deeper testing of our faith. In this test we learn that God is truly "fat," meaning He is more than able to provide for those He commands us to reach out to and also gives us a glimpse into the greatness of His provision for us as well. Abraham had to learn to discipline himself to stay focused on God and God alone while he waited for the promise of Isaac. When he took his eyes off the promise God had spoken, this is when he stumbled.

~

WE COULD HAVE PRESSED ON IN OUR OWN STRENGTH TO STAY ON OUR MANMADE TIMETABLE TO COMPLETE THE CONSTRUCTION OF THE NEW CHURCH, BUT WE WOULD NOT HAVE BEEN IN STEP WITH GOD.

~

As with the case of Lazarus in John 11:6-7, so was it with us. The raising of Lazarus from the dead by Jesus was preceded by one of Jesus' "on purpose" delays. "So, when He heard that he was sick, He stayed two more days in the place where He was. Then after this He said to the disciples, 'Let us go to Judea again.'" Jesus had this all worked out. He was stalling along the way so that His glory would be seen. "This sickness is not unto death, but for the glory of God, that the Son of God may be glorified through it." (John 11:4) Jesus raised Lazarus after a delay. Please understand this: Jesus' delays and seeming foot dragging are a sure sign of greater glory to come.

We could have pressed on in our own strength to stay on our manmade timetable to complete the construction of the new church, but we would not have been in step with God. He wanted to show forth His glory through our obedience. If we refuse to let God work in the supernatural leading and dimensions that we do not fully understand, then we really don't have any part of Him. In these times we must continue to ask, seek, and knock. We are to be found watching and listening for Him.

When we enter into seasons of waiting, it is most important that we do not fall into temptation to fall asleep from grief and weariness. Matthew 25:1-13 tells the parable of the ten virgins. This parable is enveloped in the backdrop of the great delay...waiting for the bridegroom's return. Matthew 25:5 says "But while the bridegroom was delayed, they all slumbered and slept." Know that you have heard God's Voice. Stay focused and awake...yet fully yielded to His timing and His way that He may receive the greatest glory possible through it all. Do not lose your heart for the vision and mission God has purposed for you and do not surrender your strength of mind and will. God's ways and timing are perfect. Walk on in deep trust and steady confidence.

THOUGHTS TO PONDER

♦ Are you living with a plan B mentality in the wing?

♦ Are you comfortable with the apparent delays in your life?

♦ "Aggressive yieldedness" to God supercedes our plans and schedules. Is your church in this position of "aggressive yieldedness"? Are you?

♦ What can you do right now to keep yourself focused on Jesus and the vision He has put in your heart? What can those who are yoked together in a vision do to stay focused?

THREE

~

SPARKS OF REFINING FIRE

Our journey continued on. 1989 was a year that was to bring a tremendous shifting. In fact, the tide was about to turn.

Many times in my life, the Lord has chosen to show me things; I mean literally show me things in my spirit. I will see scenes, pictures, something like little plays in my mind. It will have nothing to do usually with what I have been thinking about.

In I Samuel 9:9, Samuel is called a "seer." He, too, saw things that God wanted him to see in the spiritual realm. He was a prophet. I, in no way consider myself that, but just someone God speaks to through seeing things.

It was nearing Christmas. In fact, on the night of this happening, I was alone, as Stephen and the kids had gone out Christmas shopping. I had had a dream several nights before that something physically was wrong with my brother. In my dream, he looked paralyzed, unable to walk, and needing to be carried. In the dream, his head had fallen to one side as if he could not control the muscles in his neck.

I was deeply troubled by this dream and had called my mother and sister-in-law to see if anything was wrong with my brother, Paul. Everyone reassured me that he was in good health and getting ready for the Christmas holidays.

While Stephen and the children were out, I decided to take advantage of the quiet and have a season of prayer. As I sat before the Lord praying over this troubling dream, the phone rang. It was my mother telling me that the dream I had had, must have been from the Lord as Paul had just had a sudden heart attack. My heart sank to my feet.

In the next few days, I tried desperately to raise the money to fly home, but the tickets at that time to fly to Maine, were rather steep. I couldn't raise the money. I knew in my spirit that the Lord was going to take him home. Sure enough, in just a few days, he had gone to be with the Lord.

Later in talking with my family, they too realized the Lord had been forewarning and preparing us for his home going. Paul was a Vietnam veteran. He had been wounded three times and left for dead at least twice. His body was wracked with Agent Orange and tiny pieces of metal which surfaced up through the skin of his back until the day he died. Paul had served as a helicopter crew chief. He had a tumor on his brain from a bad hit on a helicopter gun rail during a crash. He daily struggled with jungle rot which was an irritating, burning rash that broke out at the smallest start of perspiration.

I believe God was telling me, if Paul had lived many more years, he would not have had quality of life. My brother could not have lived like that and been truly happy. He was ready to go. So at 41 years of age, Paul went home to be with the Lord.

I went back to Maine for the funeral and helped my family do the necessary things to bury him. I felt like part of my own body had been cut off. It's a different sense of sorrow and grieving when you lose a sibling. You begin to catch a glimpse of your own mortality. It feels like many chapters of your life have been abruptly ended, whether there ever was an appropriate ending written for them or not.

~

IT FEELS LIKE MANY CHAPTERS OF YOUR LIFE HAVE BEEN ABRUPTLY ENDED, WHETHER THERE EVER WAS AN APPROPRIATE ENDING WRITTEN FOR THEM OR NOT.

~

Sometimes, it seems in the passing of a loved one or friend, that the loss is eased somehow supernaturally by the Spirit of God, yet in Paul's passing, I couldn't seem to grab on to that healing flow I needed from the Lord to go through the grieving process I knew was normal. In fact, I had always been able to write songs of praise and thanks-giving to the Lord, yet at this time, I became bottled up, and absolutely nothing would flow out of my spirit. It was like my inner being went into a dark hibernation. This wasn't a very good state to be in for what was about to happen next.

Upon arriving back home from Paul's funeral, we saw the building progress was going forward. Deacon still seemed very assured that his big business deal was going to come through. Others kept giving and sacrificing. Everyone was extremely excited and on board as the desig-nated crews kept working on the new building. In fact, Deacon told his men who were working on the project, to go ahead and charge what they needed to complete the ongoing project through his companies and when the money came through, he could be reimbursed.

Different work crews from among the church folk had been developed, according to their skills and aptitude. Even the women and children were assigned tasks. I had been assigned to the electrical team and had been taught how to run electrical wires. It seemed rather comical that I would be put on this team as I was not skilled in any form of construction and I barely knew how to replace a light bulb. Yet within time, I came to enjoy working with wires and above all, the other team members. There was always a great sense of camaraderie and group accomplishment when a room or other part of a project was finished. Others were given various jobs, with team leaders supervising who were trained in those specific skills.

Everyone had a heart to work and we knew we were saving a lot of money by doing the work ourselves. It was moving to see even the young children doing simple tasks or the older saints cleaning and preparing lunches and drinks for the workers. Everyone played an important part in the construction process. Many nights the midnight oil was burned.

The date of April 1990 had been set as our target date to finish the new facility. At first, the design for the front had been drawn out all in stone. One of the men in the church had a stone quarrying business and he had designed a beautifully finished front for the church. His own business ran on a tight budget, and even though in his heart he had wanted to complete the project, he had trouble meeting the deadlines and furnishing the stone. At that time, a plan B was developed and another stone mason was hired to finish the church in stone and brick combined. The finished job still looked great!

Stephen, during this time period, became like Nehemiah. Nehemiah had said to the people in Nehemiah 2:18, "'Let us rise up and build.' Then they set their hands to this good work." He and others were spending all day and most of their evenings working at the church. He is a finish carpenter, and his skills were badly needed to help move the work along. Also, his leadership in rallying and assigning the people to various work crews was of the utmost importance.

Carl was another one of the main anchors that helped to keep the project on task. The two of them continued to burn the midnight oil many nights and then got up early the next morning and did the same thing all over again the next day.

There were other precious men and women from the church body, who were giving every free moment to help work towards the completion of the church. We became like those told about in Nehemiah 3:23. It says, "So neither I, my brethren, my servants, nor the men of the guard who followed me took off our clothes, except that everyone took them off for washing." Our hearts were truly in a position to finish what the Lord had spoken to us so clearly during those days of fasting and prayer.

During this time period, one of the men working closely with Stephen, began to see a falling away of sorts, a cooling off in Deacon. Carl had been asked to pray with him several times because Deacon had been feeling ill. It seemed to Carl, that the heart of Deacon was turning back towards Egypt, (becoming more interested and distracted by other things), just small telltale signs, but some warning signs none the less.

The Lord had been dealing with Deacon for years about brokenness. He had spoken often about it, even teaching this topic in his adult Sunday school class. I believe there was a season in his life, when he had desired it in a very great way, yet, I'm sure there were many temptations laid out before him subtly and slyly by the enemy of his soul. You see, he, the old serpent from the beginning, didn't like the idea of an on fire church, building in his own back yard, and right outside of this big city. He didn't like the thought that this church had a heart for lost, hurting souls and had the gumption and audacity to pray and work to see a great harvest won into the kingdom of God. He had to come up with a clever master plan to try and halt the work of the Lord. His many seeds of doubt that he had secretly been planting, were slowly beginning to take root. He just needed to find the right soil to work in.

~

HIS MANY SEEDS OF DOUBT THAT HE HAD SECRETLY BEEN PLANTING, WERE SLOWLY BEGINNING TO TAKE ROOT. HE JUST NEEDED TO FIND THE RIGHT SOIL TO WORK IN.

~

Looking back now, I realize one of the biggest mistakes we made in going into this building project, was not having the adequate prayer covering so desperately needed for the spiritual warfare that was to come, as well as the physical warfare we were going to encounter. We hadn't yet learned the important lesson that Nehemiah 4:16 teaches us. It says, "So it was, from that time on, that half of my servants worked at construction, while the other half held the spears, the shields, the bows, and wore armor; and the leaders were behind all the house of Judah." Verse 18 continues on, saying, "Every one of the builders had his sword girded at his side as he built. And the one who sounded the trumpet was beside me." We sorely learned an extremely hard lesson by not having a team of seasoned intercessors standing, day and night, in that place of prayer that was required for this huge undertaking.

Never again will this happen in our ministry. We, beyond a doubt, have learned that "we do not wrestle against flesh and blood, but principalities, against powers, against the rulers of the darkness of this age, against spiritual hosts of wickedness in the heavenly place," Ephesians 6:12.

It says in Nehemiah 4:20 that Nehemiah told them, "Wherever you hear the sound of the trumpet, rally to us there. Our God will fight for us." As we ran into challenges along the way, we should have been calling this special team of intercessors to cover it all in fervent prayer.

When one of us would come under attack, we should have sounded the trumpet and began to make intercession for them and fight off the fiery darts of the wicked one. I am sure this is one of the most important lessons the Lord was going to continue teaching my husband and me over the years to come. Pray, pray, pray and when you don't know what to do after that...pray some more!

We were about to enter on a treacherous leg of our journey, like Joseph, who also had had a dream, never thinking it would go the way it did. If we had been asked to write a hypothetical outline of how we thought our life's work would have gone, absolutely none of what we were about to experience would have been included. Who ever makes plans for entering an "ordained prison"? Who ever wants to be kept in this "ordained prison", during the prime of their lives? Yet, God was working out His detailed plan.

~

WHO EVER WANTS TO BE KEPT IN THIS "ORDAINED PRISON", DURING THE PRIME OF THEIR LIVES? YET, GOD WAS WORKING OUT HIS DETAILED PLAN.

~

We, like Joseph, were about to have every minute area of our lives, inward and outward sifted and deeply challenged. Where we thought we were strong, we would find out we were weak. And likewise, where we thought we were weak, we would find we were strong.

"For You, O God, have tested us; You have refined us as silver is refined," Psalm 66:10.

"Behold, I have refined you, but not as silver; I have tested you in the furnace of affliction," Isaiah 48:10.

"I will bring the one-third through the fire, will refine them as silver is refined, and test them as gold is tested. They will call on My Name, and I will answer them. I will say, 'This is My people; and each one will say, 'The LORD is my God,'" Zechariah 13:9.

"But who can endure the day of His coming? And who can stand when He appears? For He is like a refiner's fire and like launderer's soap. He will sit as a refiner and a purifier of silver; He will purify the sons of Levi, and purge them as gold and silver, that they may offer to the LORD an offering in righteousness," Malachi 3:2-3.

We were soon to enter the crucible of the refining process of God. If I had known then what we were about to go through, I would have run as fast as I could in the opposite direction. Yet God was working His plan.

~ PERSONAL REFLECTIONS ~

Make no mistake, God's tremendous shifting and sudden turn of the tides in your life are a fire. God will not allow us to mutate into a lukewarm, insipid, self-centered, powerless form of religion. Revelation 3:14-22 gives the qualities of the end-time Laodicean church. They were lukewarm, having a form of godliness but no power. How does God deal with this within us? He allows fires to put the heat on our lives: physical distress, family distress, financial distress. Without the heat we grow cold. Some may say this cannot be from God because He has given us specific promises in His Word that He will deliver us. He does deliver us, but He uses the time while we are waiting on His way out of the trial to cleanse and purify by the heat of fiery trial. The mercy of God is shown to you through the fiery distress you face.

Psalm 105:16-22 says "Moreover, He called for a famine upon the land (of Egypt); He cut off every source of bread. He sent a man before them, even Joseph, who was sold as a servant. His feet they hurt with fetters; he was laid in chains of iron and his soul entered into the iron, until his word (to his cruel brothers) came true, until the word of the Lord tried and tested him. The king sent and loosed him, even the ruler of the peoples, and let him go free. He made Joseph lord of his house and ruler of all his substance. To bind his princes at his pleasure and teach his elders wisdom." Some translations render verse 18 "His soul came into iron." I believe that Joseph's imprisonment was not just in a physical sense. It also was literally a chaining of his soul. These words conjure up pictures of great mental anguish. "Until the time that his word came to pass, the word of the Lord tested him." Joseph's dream had been that his father, his mother, and his brothers would all bow down before him. He carried a dream—a word from God in his heart. While the manifestation of that word was held off, that very word "tested him." It was this kind of fire that was the makings of the man. Joseph had learned to wait patiently for God to fulfill His purpose. He had yielded himself to the process of God in allowing God to mature him. He came to the place where he could function as a mature co-laborer with Him.

~

HE HAD YIELDED HIMSELF TO THE PROCESS OF GOD IN ALLOWING GOD TO MATURE HIM.

~

Joseph did not allow himself to fall into the trap of reminiscing and becoming overly nostalgic. This is a major curve ball the enemy will throw at us to suck us into a vortex of depression. There are many seasons in our lives, each rich with treasure to be purchased from the Lord. Even if we could go back to a past time, it truly would never be the same as when we actually lived it. Full trust for the present time is a learned practice. One does not get this revelation early in life. In looking backwards while driving forward, we often miss all of the beauty the Lord has prepared for us today and for this exact season.

Luke 14:28 says, "For which of you, wishing to build a farm building, does not first sit down and calculate the cost (to see) whether he has sufficient means to finish it?" We had surely counted the financial cost of this building project but had sadly not counted the cost in anointed prayer covering. Any and all projects whether large or small, need to be taken before the Lord daily, asking God to cover every detail of it. We were very presumptuous in our thinking that just because we were doing the work of the Lord, He would take care of everything without us specifically seeking Him about it. How wrong we were! God desires us to include Him in absolutely every part. Nothing is to be overlooked as far as submitting it all to the Father for His direction and blessing.

We should have assigned the most seasoned intercessors to daily prayer. This should have been their job throughout the whole process—nothing else but waiting on the Lord for this chosen time. Along with the pastors, these should have been the ones in the spiritual watchtowers of prayer looking for the attacks of the enemy and for new revelations in prayer all the length of our journey in taking new territory for the kingdom. Ezekiel 22:30 says, "And I sought a man among them who should build up the wall and stand in the gap before Me for the land, that I should not destroy it, but I found none." Intercessors are a vital part of moving forward in the vision and minute plans of

~

WHEN YOU ENTER THE VALLEY YOU WILL LEARN THAT YOU ARE NOT LIFTED OUT OF THE VALLEY; YOU GROW THROUGH THE VALLEY.

~

God. This does not mean that we all shouldn't be praying; we should. But there are those among us who have a definite calling to pray and a unique anointing and gifting to intercede as the Spirit of the Lord would lead. These are the ones we must ask to cover us in whatever endeavor we take in the Lord. "Philippians 4:6 says, "Do not fret or have any anxiety about anything, but in every circumstance and in everything, by prayer and petition (definite requests), with thanksgiving, continue to make your wants known to God." Ephesians 6:18 says, "Pray at all times (on every occasion, in every season) in the Spirit, with all (manner of) prayer and entreaty. To that end keep alert and watch with strong purpose and perseverance, interceding in behalf of all the saints (God's consecrated people)." Our naïve youth and young strength failed to recognize our total dependence upon the Lord. Sadly, our loss—the enemy's gain.

When you enter the valley you will learn that you are not lifted out of the valley; you grow **through** the valley. The Lord will take great care to straighten out in our lives what we have not even thought to ask. One can minister almost exclusively by his spiritual perception. God has always spoken and given clarity and direction this way in the past by the ability to see spiritually. The sense of sight is so powerful, this is easy to do. Yet God wants to develop in us our sense of spiritual hearing as well. And to do this He shut down our sense of seeing spiritually by now introducing a season of darkness. There is absolutely nothing wrong with seeing things in the Spirit. But it is wrong to presume that is all there is. There is more to the spiritual realm than what one can discern only with the spiritual eye alone. The eye and the ear have different functions and perceive things differently. God will take us into seasons where we will see absolutely nothing but we will hear His voice at these times of darkness. Romans 4:17 tells us that God calls those things that are not as though they were. We don't see these things, but we hear the voice of calling speaking these things and we recognize it is Him. This is the beginning of the refining process. The flesh says run...the Spirit says stand still.

THOUGHTS TO PONDER

♦ "The mercy of God is shown to you through the fiery distress you face." Is this a comfort to you or a challenge to your thinking?

♦ "This kind of fire was the makings of the man." Can one mature to their full potential without "this kind of fire"?

♦ "He yielded himself to the process of God in allowing God to mature him. He came to the place where he could function as a mature co-laborer with Him." Are you aggressively yielded to God in His maturing process in your life?

♦ Reminiscing and becoming overly nostalgic can lead to depression. Is this hard to recognize? Is enjoying and resting in all the different seasons of growth possible?

♦ Discuss the importance of seasoned intercessors being on duty for both physical and spiritual building projects.

♦ Discuss the importance of developing spiritual hearing as well as spiritual sight.

FOUR

~

WHAT A TANGLED
WEB WE WEAVE...

Jeremiah 23:29 says, "Is not My word like a fire?" says the Lord, "and like a hammer that breaks the rock in pieces?" The picture that comes to my mind as I read this Scripture is that of God picking a person up by these big tongs and holding them over His fiery furnace, waiting until they are red hot, then putting them on His anvil and hammering them into shape. I now know that this process of God includes pain, loss of control, violent change, and intense pressure.

I am reminded that even Jesus' eyes are of fire and that they pierce through every layer of our being, exposing the true condition of our hearts. He sees us as we really are, and not how we perceive ourselves to be in our own self-righteousness.

In his adult Sunday school class, Deacon began to openly question if it was the timing of the Lord for us to finish the new building and move the church. Of course, it was always said as a hypothetical question, never supposedly truly wanting to cast doubt and wavering in others' hearts, but yet (whether knowing or unknowingly), this was what was happening. Whenever he would help officiate in services, he would questioningly speak things that began to plant tiny seeds of fear in hearts as to whether we were really ready to move. His implication was that he had doubts as to the congregation's and leadership's spiritual maturity.

The devil was so slick. Deacon continued to speak about brokenness and really, beneath his words, was implying that none of us had truly ever been broken by the Lord. Therefore, in his estimation, we were not ready to move.

In Revelation 2:20 Jesus speaks to the church of Thyatira with these words, "But I have this against you: that you tolerate the woman Jezebel, who calls herself a prophetess (claiming to be inspired), and who is teaching and leading astray my servants and beguiling them." Jezebel had no intention to strengthen the unity of the church of Thyatira. She had every intention of usurping authority. Why would we be so naïve to think if the enemy could work through someone such as her in the church of Thyatira in the New Testament age, why wouldn't he still be up to his old tricks today? Even as the serpent was very subtle in the Garden of Eden, so he appeared on the stage of our lives.

~

WHY WOULD WE BE SO NAÏVE TO THINK IF THE ENEMY COULD WORK THROUGH SOMEONE SUCH AS HER IN THE CHURCH OF THYATIRA IN THE NEW TESTAMENT AGE, WHY WOULDN'T HE STILL BE UP TO HIS OLD TRICKS TODAY?

~

Deacon started to make some new efforts to raise funds to continue the building project as his big business deal had not come through as he had planned. It seems he asked different companies that he and his family members owned to give a tithe from their businesses. Stephen and others implored him not to try to make the building project happen, but let the Lord provide as He would choose, in

His timing and way. There were several times when others tried to talk to Deacon, stating it would be fine to let the project sit for awhile and for us to wait on the Lord for further provision.

Deacon began to tell others what a tremendous amount of strain he was under and stated that he had never really ever had to take a step of faith. Yet, he said it seemed to him that the church and his jobs were bringing such anxiety, it would kill him. He talked as if he was totally alone in everything, that he alone was carrying all the responsibility and doing all the work. Probably this was how he perceived it at the time, however untrue it really was.

No one had ever made Deacon the general contractor of the project. He was an important team player, to be sure, but it never was meant for him to become a one man band. It was to have been a group effort, with everyone doing their part. Leadership repeatedly tried to get him not to give financially into the project any more than he felt comfortable with. Yet, there seemed to be a mistaken sense of great power and control in him causing him to feel that it was his responsibility to see the project finished. No one except him, with his wife over the finances, had a clear picture of what he was giving or how he was moving funds around without others knowledge.

In August, 1990, we had run out of all the money that had been raised to date. Deacon came to the building committee and stated he thought it wise to go to a bank and take out a bullet loan for two hundred thousand dollars anticipating the money from his big deal would come through, and then the bullet loan would be paid off. He would be co-signing it with the church so there would be no problem in getting it.

Shortly before this was to happen, Stephen felt strongly impressed by the Lord to go to Deacon and encourage him to sign the deed to the new property over to the church and have it legally put under the church's name. It had never been done in the months previous to this. Deacon deeded only enough to build on, but not the entire piece that had been shown to Stephen by the Lord. Only the piece of land on which the church was being built was deeded over, which was 5+ acres. Deacon promised another 12 acres along with this portion. He assured Pastor that he would take care of the deeding of that piece of land later.

Deacon over the years had had his hands in a lot of different building projects with his businesses, etc. Specifically though, he was never given the position of general contractor or builder over the church project. There were several gifted men who knew construction who were working together as a team in completing the project. Everyone was using their specific talents to help.

Deacon had put some of his men, (when he didn't have other jobs for them), working on the church construction. At this time, as his own businesses began to get busy, he began to pull his workers off the job to do other projects. Now the work on the house of God began to really slow down to a crawl.

Deacon began to openly question whether Stephen and I had even been called to pastor the church and openly began to state that he wondered if we could handle pastoring the new church in this new location. We would hear stories of things he was saying, yet we didn't want to believe our ears.

During the past nine years of ministry, I had led the youth and been worship leader. I had worked in the school and wherever I was needed. Deacon had the adept ability to make me feel like queen for the day, in one moment giving glowing praise, and then in another breath, he could make me feel that I belonged at the absolute bottom of the manure pile. I would become nervous around him, especially in committee meetings because I never knew which way the wind was going to blow. Unstable is one word you could use to describe his behavior.

~

WHENEVER YOU WALK AROUND SOMEONE LIKE YOU ARE WALKING ON EGG SHELLS, KNOW IT IS NOT A THING OF GOD.

~

Deacon was a master at manipulation. I now know that Satan uses this to control and hold power over others' lives. Whenever you walk around someone like you are walking on eggshells, know it is not a thing of God. It actually is a form of witchcraft. God wants people to walk before Him out of a willing heart that is transparent and open before all men. Peace should reign in relationships, not fear, always feeling sick to your stomach and all nerved up whenever you have to be around them. We don't have to control and hold others in fear to get what we want or think is the right thing. We can trust God to bring about His purposes. We were young and inexperienced, green to be exact. We had never experienced this kind of turmoil before. God was teaching us some very hard lessons along these lines that we would never forget.

During the spring of 1990, some inner situations within the school with one new teacher began to erupt. She was one who had had no experience teaching but felt she knew how all the other teachers should be functioning. She took it upon herself to do a written evaluation of each one and seeing that it got placed in their hands. She proclaimed herself as being so compassionate to a few children who had challenges learning and made leadership and others out to be uncaring and unconcerned. She set herself up as a little savior with all the answers and only she supposedly was flowing in God's love. It seems the devil always will have a few willing vessels to work his mischief through.

II Timothy 3:6, 7 says "For among them are those who worm their way into homes and captivate silly and weak-natured and spiritually dwarfed women, loaded down (the burden of their) sins (and easily) swayed and led away by various evil desires and seductive impulses. These weak women will listen to anybody who will teach them); they are forever inquiring and getting information, but are never able to arrive at a recognition and knowledge of the Truth."

This began to happen. It wasn't everyone. It never is. It usually is a person that is seemingly spiritual and religious. You see the enemy will come disguised in a religious spirit also. This isn't the Spirit of God. It is the spirit of Satan. He is the father of lies. He looks for willing, "religious" people to speak his lies through. He found a few among us, this specific teacher being one.

~

IT WASN'T EVERYONE. IT NEVER IS.
IT USUALLY IS A PERSON THAT IS
SEEMINGLY SPIRITUAL AND RELIGIOUS.

~

These were people being influenced whom we had pastored for nine years, faithfully loving them and ministering to them and their families. Now this small few began telling outright lies they knew were not to be true, in order to come to some wanted end known only to them.

Once again I was to feel the lashing tongue of Deacon. I was now principal of the school and was the one who was trying to settle disputes, bring unity and resolve the misunderstandings that had taken place. Oh, what a dirt bag I had become! I wish you could have been a little mouse in the corner that day as I was dressed down verbally! Verbal abuse would be a term I would use, but it would be an understatement. How could someone speak such cruel accusations with not one thought of common sense in them or how hurtful and scarring their words were?

I'm sure if you are in a position of leadership, you know how vicious the devil can be! Oh, how he loves to intimidate and discourage the servant of the Lord if given the chance! The devil had the ball rolling now. Just what he wanted!

When Satan gets a snowball rolling, he isn't one to let it lose momentum. In September of 1990, Deacon met with some of the men in leadership to drop a major bombshell. He was there to tell them that a petition had been brought to him by some discontents, to have the denominational district officials brought in concerning allegations about the pastor and his wife. But, let's not lose sight that God is in all of this...somewhere. I knew in my head that Isaiah 43:2 says, "When you pass through the waters, I will be with you, and through the rivers, they will not overwhelm you. When you walk through the fire, you will not be burned or scorched, nor will the flame kindle upon you." All I knew was that it was surely getting mighty hot and I could smell the stench of smoke all around me.

As human nature goes, groups were formed and unbeknownst to us, Deacon conveniently became the covering for the whole group of discontents. Many of the church family had not even heard of a petition or any disgruntlement that was moving. It was only a few, stirred up by innuendoes and lascivious gossip. But, it was enough live ammunition for the wretched enemy to keep on what he had been deviously planning for a long while.

At this time, work on the church had all but ceased, except for a few volunteers. The enemy was trying to crudely rip the very God-given vision out of the sincere hearts of the people. If Satan would have had it his way, that's exactly what would have happened.

My old pastor used to say, "Never close both eyes." I never quite understood that saying until this mountain of crushing hurt came crashing down on us. 1 Peter 5:8 says,

"Be sober, be vigilant; because your adversary the devil walks about like a roaring lion, seeking whom he may devour." Wow, could he ever roar! And he seemed to be able to hit you right where it hurt, in the very center of the bull's eye...your tender love for God's people.

~

IF CHRIST HAD TO SUFFER, WHY WOULDN'T WE?

~

1 Peter 5:9,10 goes on to say, "Resist him, steadfast in the faith, knowing that the same sufferings are experienced by your brotherhood in the world. But may the God of all grace, who called us to His eternal glory by Christ Jesus, after you have suffered a while, perfect, establish, strengthen, and settle you." Hum...after you have suffered awhile. Something just never would settle in my spirit right when I would hear television preachers and others say that we were never going to suffer. It didn't make a lot of sense to me. If Christ had to suffer, why wouldn't we? In the months and years to come, we would grow to understand these Scriptures in depth a whole lot better.

~ PERSONAL REFLECTIONS ~

Pastors in developing nations suffer persecution on a regular basis. Their persecution often comes from other religions and cults. It seems to me that much of the persecution in America comes from within the church, not unlike the days that Christ lived and ministered in. The religious spirit is still alive and well today, still doing as much damage as possible.

It is wrong to not instruct and teach young men and women coming out of our colleges, ready to begin their ministries about such persecution. They are being sent out ill equipped with rose colored glasses firmly planted on their faces. They seem more interested in their "packages" and what "perks" will be theirs than getting a solid warning and caution given on how to just survive their particular calling. We must believe the Spirit of God to arise, train and equip leaders and impart powerful discernment and tenacity to them to stand their ground and posts and not yield in any way to the devil himself.

THOUGHTS TO PONDER

♦ How do you recognize someone who sows discord among the brethren? Discuss how someone can appear as an "angel of light." (See 2 Corinthians 11:14)

♦ What affect does "power and control" have on an individual? What affect does it have on those around them?

♦ Power, control, intimidation...can these be called symptoms of witchcraft, a religious spirit?

♦ Discuss this statement, "We don't have to control and hold others in fear to get what we want or think is the right thing. We can trust God to bring about His purposes."

♦ Discuss the personal repercussions of this statement, "Wow, could he ever roar. And he seemed to be able to hit you right where it hurt, in the very center of the bull's eye...your tender love for God's people."

♦ Discuss: If Christ had to suffer, why wouldn't we? What about the suffering of others in persecuted lands?

FIVE

~

PROPHETIC DREAMS

As I have stated before, God often speaks to me in dreams. Sometimes I would have a dream that would give us specific direction. Often the Lord would cause me to dream a dream that He wanted me to share with someone else as a means of encouragement to them. Just as Joseph was given a dream concerning his future, (Genesis 37:5) even so, God still speaks to us today.

I was soon to find out that He also gives dreams of warning, preparing our hearts for a trial we are about to walk through. The sense in my spirit of why He does this is to let us know He knows all about it before it is to come to pass and that He is in total control. Genesis 41:1-7 tells us that Pharaoh dreamed a dream that was warning him of an upcoming famine in Egypt. Within the dream, was also the answer to the warning. God used Joseph to interpret the dream and opened the way for him to be exalted as one of the primary leaders over Egypt.

Sometimes, dreams can be given as conditional. For example, if you will do this, then this will happen. If you don't do this, then this will happen. The choice of outcome is determined in God's eyes by our reaction to the warning. I believe there are times He simply is warning us of something that is going to happen and there is nothing we can or cannot do to change it. He simply wants us prepared and wholly trusting Him through it.

Several weeks before the massive attack of the enemy was released upon us and the church, I had such a dream. I dreamt that I was in a small fun park. I was on a brightly colored merry-go-round, riding a painted horse, just going around and around. In the dream, my attention was drawn to something beneath the ride. I kept looking intently down below the carousal as it went round and round.

There was lush, green foliage underneath it. The thought kept coming to me in the dream that someone was trying to craftily hide something important underneath this lush foliage. As I continued to go around and around, I kept piercing intently down, trying to see into this dense greenery. Something was hidden I could not see.

Then the scene changed. I saw Mildred and Gene, a couple from our church, sitting in a little trailer, the kind that people live in who are working in a carnival. They were chatting and relaxing, when unexpectedly they got up and pulled out the little couch they were sitting on away from the wall. Behind it, they found a paper bag. They looked bewildered as to why that would be hiding behind the couch. I remember seeing them looking into the bag and then looking at each other with shocked expressions on their faces.

Then the scene changed. I was now on a wooden boardwalk. Up ahead of me was Deacon, with what looked like the trousers of a sailor's uniform, yet with just a white T-shirt on for his top. He wasn't in a full sailor's uniform, although that looked like what he intended to be wearing. He was running away trying to hide a brown paper bag. I couldn't figure out why he was trying to hide this from me.

Finally, the dream came to an end with me seeing this bigger than life china doll. It too was fully dressed in a sailor's outfit. The china doll had long, blonde curls, and yet its blue eyes were more than just regular doll's eyes. As I looked into those eyes I could see they were hideously filled with evil.

The doll, as fast as lightning, snatched up my right hand, which somehow struck me as odd, seeing I am left handed. (I later was to find out that the right hand is the hand used as a symbol of authority.)

I don't know how to explain what happened next, other than to try. Even though I was dreaming, I literally, physically, could feel this evil doll as it grabbed my hand and tried to pierce a whole into my palm. Its eyes were locked with mine! As the stabbing pain continued to radiate through my hand and up my arm, the doll said in a growling slow voice, "I hate you! I hate you! I hate you!"

I never will forget the odd eeriness I felt as I looked straight back into those demonic eyes. The embodiment of hell itself was in that mesmerizing doll.

I awoke abruptly. I was soaking wet in the very throws of a cold sweat. Shaking Stephen, he soon awakened. Both of us could discern easily that this horrid dream was a warning that something was up. Immediately, while sitting in our bed that night, we went into intercessory prayer, asking God to give us His much needed understanding and wisdom. Oh, the dark evil that looms in the heart of Satan and every willing vessel he can find to work through. We, all too soon, would have a full understanding of this monstrous dream.

Around the same time, Stephen had a dream that he was in a boat, paddling while standing up in the front of the boat. The sense he had in the dream was to keep his face set like a flint and not to stop paddling.

In his dream, there was a woven basket sitting in the middle of the boat. Suddenly, out of the basket lunged a big snake, rising, and poised ready to strike him from behind. Then in the dream a white mongoose appeared. The mongoose attacked the snake putting up a powerful fight, wounding and disarming the snake. The snake continued to viciously attack the mongoose to the place where it looked like the mongoose could never survive.

The mongoose appeared to be breathing very heavily, with its chest heaving in and out. It had bandages wrapped around it, yet blood was seeping through because of such deep wounds. The thought came to Stephen in the dream that this mongoose was never going to make it.

~

I BELIEVE GOD WOULD SPEAK TO US
THIS WAY MORE OFTEN IF WE WOULD TAKE
SERIOUSLY WHAT HE IS TRYING TO SHOW US.

~

Both the snake and the mongoose sat there for awhile as Stephen just continued to steadily paddle the boat down the river.

All of a sudden, the snake rose to strike again. This time around, there was no more strength in the wounded mongoose to fight. It looked like the end for the brave mongoose.

Incredibly, out of the sky appeared a powerful eagle. The eagle majestically swept down attacking the poised, striking snake. The eagle killed the wicked snake and tore it into pieces devouring it.

Stephen then had what appeared to be an Eskimo parka with a fur trimmed hood bordering his face suddenly placed down over him. As this coat came around him, the mongoose turned into a woman who also was wearing the same type of Eskimo parka. She stepped up beside him in a parallel stance. She began to help paddle the boat up the river. Both their faces were set like flint.

It is important to journal your dreams. I believe God would speak to us this way more often if we would take seriously what He is trying to show us. I carefully wrote down every detail and we together began to seek the Lord for understanding. Even though these dreams were warnings, it was comforting to know that He already knew what was going to happen and that He knew the way that we were to take.

In months and years to come, God would clearly give the interpretation of this dream. I thank Him for His reassurance that He gives at exactly the needed moment especially as we walk through those frightening dark places in our lives.

~ PERSONAL REFLECTIONS ~

I believe that God wants and would reveal more to us supernaturally if we would only allow Him to. We have exercised our natural senses to pick up the slightest odor or sound; we are able to tell in an instant what a particular taste is. Yet our spiritual senses seem dull in comparison to our natural senses. What if Joseph had chosen to ignore Pharaoh's dreams and write them off as an Egyptian pizza dream? Israel and Egypt would have found themselves in some serious trouble. How many times has God tried to warn us, or encourage us or direct us but we did not heed the dream or the vision or the repeated sense of the Holy Spirit in our hearts? What could we have been spared from if we only had exercised our spiritual senses to a greater place of maturity in the Lord?

~

WHAT IF JOSEPH HAD CHOSEN TO IGNORE PHARAOH'S DREAMS AND WRITE THEM OFF AS AN EGYPTIAN PIZZA DREAM?

~

Peter had to step out of the boat to follow Jesus. He did this by faith. I believe the Lord is telling us that if we want to follow Him, we will have to step out of the boat. It's a completely supernatural walk.

From hindsight, looking back we understand that Deacon was scheming his attack plans. He was hiding his thoughts and moves from us and all leadership who would not fall in with him. The evil doll I believe, was symbolizing the demonic attacks that would be loosed against us. They definitely were filled with hate and did not want us to grow into the place of authority God had destined for us. Deacon and the doll wearing the same type of clothing represented that they were in cahoots together, of the same spirit.

Stephen's dream showed us that there would be several attacks. As we sought the Lord concerning the mongoose, we felt it was me, that I would almost die whether physically or spiritually under the attacks, but that I would survive and be able to stand beside him in ministry with our faces set like a flint.

Sometimes it is hard to discern God's timetable from man's. Yet we know that we can safely trust Him. We continue to this day, listening carefully and expectantly for every word that would proceed from the mouth of God no matter how it may come to us.

THOUGHTS TO PONDER

♦ Is it important to pay attention to your dreams? How can you get out of balance in this area?

♦ If you do not understand the dream, how do you get the understanding? Does prayer play an important roll in this?

♦ Is there enough teaching today concerning how to receive and understand the Voice of God through visions and dreams?

SIX

TREACHERY IN
THE MAKING

In October of the same year, a building committee meeting had been called by the pastor to try and sort things out. Of course, no one was comfortable now with each other. No one except a very few knew what was truly going on. Stephen was deeply hurt and upset over Deacon's verbal abuse to me. No normal man was going to take this kind of harsh treatment of his wife sitting down. We have come to learn after the fact that Deacon had a reputation for verbally being abusive to the former pastors and their wives when he became upset and wanted to gain back control of the pastor. His tongue would become the cutting whip. Why not try it again now? Needless to say, the meeting got very heated and during it, Stephen made the suggestion to Deacon that it may be better if he and his band of bothered discontents stay in the present facility and he become their pastor.

Now I'm not suggesting here that my husband had heard a word from the Lord. There is a difference between a young man's strength and zeal in comparison to an older, more seasoned man of God and their thinking and actions tempered under the direction of the Holy Spirit. An older man may have taken this kind of verbal punishment more gracefully, yet I have learned after listening to many older pastors who have walked through similar things, it seems if you don't stand up to this kind of attack of the enemy in some way, you usually get steam rolled right over.

Yet, remember, God was in this…somewhere. You feel when you walk through this kind of confrontation, like your world is crumbling and shattering all around you. The security and routine of happy days has flown off with the wind and you simply don't know how to get them back. Presently, you know that you have truly heard from God, and you are doing your best to work out what He has asked you to do. That's about all you could tightly cling to and try to hold on for dear life. Your emotions and reasoning told you to get up and run as fast as you could in the opposite direction. Yet the Holy Spirit somehow would shed just enough courage and hope to get you through just one more day.

Our faith at this time was not haughty, yet it was unbroken. Maybe you could say we were presumptuous. We had not yet learned that the greatest dimensions of faith can be entrusted only to vessels that are broken. This was just the beginning of sorrows for us and the beginning of our season of deeper lessons to prepare us for God's greater plan. But we couldn't see or understand that at the present moment.

~

OUR FAITH AT THIS TIME WAS NOT HAUGHTY, YET IT WAS UNBROKEN.

~

The climax of this heated meeting was that a vote was taken by the board as to whether they felt it right for Deacon and his disgruntled cohorts to stay behind in the old facility as a congregation or not. The vote was split down the middle. Oh, what a huge mess was developing now!

We still felt just as strongly to follow the leading of the Lord to go forward into the new church.

A petition of the complaining discontents was circulated and signed and sent to the denominational district office asking the superintendent to come and sit in on these meetings. Stephen and I had been with this denomination for over 13 years, faithful and true blue, holding their torch high, supporting it with our tithes, public backing and support. Only once, in the nine years we had pastored in our state, had we received a pastoral visit from our denominational covering. It's hard to build relationships with people you don't have opportunity to have fellowship with over time.

The monthly district meetings where the pastors gathered together were more or less a time to see who had moved out of the district and who had moved in. Also congregational attendance records were published monthly in the denominational paper and your success was based on how high or how low your attendance number was each month. Not much in the way of relationships or mentoring was to be had. It usually was a meeting of the chosen frozen. Everyone seemed to be wretchedly trapped behind their plastic smiles and small talk niceties. Sometimes when someone's plastic mask would slightly slip when they thought no one was looking, you would catch this brief look of longing for true fellowship and heartfelt encouragement. But then, almost as fast as it had slipped down, it was pulled right back up into place for fear someone might really be seeing what was going on inside and perceive them to be a weak loser. I would always feel a sense of restless sadness within me as we walked away from those meetings, a sense of sore disappointment over what could have been, what should have been.

The officers of the denomination were to be treated as some sort of denominational hierarchy with others fawning and desiring to become "just like them" as they tried to climb the ladder to become what? Was it title that fed into this box of thinking or was it the wider praise and acclaim of man that was the seductive snare? Where was the true leading and touch of God on a person's life that challenged others to want to know Jesus, high and lifted up and not man? Did that not count for something? We have sat in huge denominational meetings for up to half an hour in the service and listen to the roll call of "who's who" in the meeting and everyone clap and cheer.

I want to clarify that not all of those in leadership in this denomination carried themselves like this, yet there were many that did. I wonder if they were a "sweet smelling aroma" to how many here on earth, let alone in heaven. We soon were to feel the sting of their wrath also.

It became obvious to us in the very first board meeting that money and power talked with the district officials. They forthrightly sided with Deacon because of previous financial gifts and old denominational friendships Deacon's father had had with the district. His father had been the founding pastor of the church many years ago and had also been a missionary to Africa under their covering. He was a faithful man of God and had done a good work here and abroad.

In the meanwhile, members of the board decided to hear the grievances of the discontents. They met with each one and listened, trying to genuinely hear and discern what the real problems were. Their conclusion was that there wasn't anything they could understand to be major areas of difficulty. No two people had the same complaint, nor did they make much sense. The bottom line was, as stated before, that there had been silly women gossiping from house to house influenced under the affirming nod of Deacon who had always been an authority figure in their lives. He had bailed many of them out when taxes were due or helped when a new vehicle was needed and they had no money to purchase one. Their allegiance was warped by this distorted giving. There had never been any close relationship between them and Deacon, other than the fact that he could wield control over them and use them to do his bidding when needed.

Members had never really had to give into the church for any project or needs because Deacon had always taken care of it. When the church began to grow, this little group, who had always puppy dogged around after him, became less powerful along with him. This sense of not being in complete control of the congregation and the pastor was foreign to him. His teachings on brokenness seemed not to have gone very deep. In times like this, the thought would arise in me - does one serve the Lord because it meets a need in their ego or is it because they really love Him?

The conclusion of the board, after hearing all the discontents, was that there was nothing legitimate in their complaints for them to have made such a commotion. Nevertheless, a congregational meeting was called with the district superintendent coming in to chair the meeting.

Superintendent Pride walked in wearing his professional looking suit and carrying his leather briefcase, appearing to all to be very important and seemingly very spiritual. He told everyone boldly, that he had heard from God the night before and he had the master plan of how to untangle this knotted web. He allowed anyone who wanted to stand and voice how they felt to do so and tell everyone what was bothering them. The displeased discontents stood and yelled and screamed out things that could not even be understood because their words were so full of venom. I was even accused of reading pornographic material by one young woman who we had been counseling. She had become involved with a married pastor whose wife, because of this promiscuous foray, was on the verge of an emotional breakdown.

I could feel myself being drawn into an innocent imprisonment, all out of my control and power to stop. I sat there remembering the vision and dream given from the Lord for these people and thinking inwardly, "This is not what you told us, Lord." Psalm 105:19 tells us that "the word of the Lord tried and tested Joseph." This was a hard, hard thing. God Himself had tailor-made Joseph's prison and with the mix of all his setbacks and just the right carnal people involved, it created a clinging dependency deep in Joseph on God alone. I couldn't believe what I was hearing, but there it was, negative, corrupting, vile venom spewing from individuals all over others.

~

WHAT IS THIS GOLD THAT IS REFINED IN THE FIRE? THIS GOLD IS A PURIFIED FAITH.

~

The enemy of my soul was rapidly hammering away at my mind and spirit to strongly tempt me to embrace his hideous lies and become poisonously embittered. I was trying desperately to keep my heart pure before the Lord. "Grace, Lord, give me Your grace, please!" Revelation 3:18 says, "I counsel you to buy from Me gold refined in the fire, that you may be rich." What is this gold that is refined in the fire? This gold is a purified faith. I Peter 1:7 says, "That the genuineness of your faith, being much more precious than gold that perishes, though it is tested by fire, may be found to praise, honor, and glory at the revelation of Jesus Christ." When we learn to survive the fire, prayerfully we come out on the other side with a much stronger faith.

The gold also was going to refine our character. Job 23:10 says, "But He knows the way that I take; when He has tested me, I shall come forth as gold." This gold is in truth a process of bringing and growing Christ-likeness within us. True riches, we were to learn, would come as we learned to walk through fiery trials that in His great wisdom, God would use to conform us to the image of Jesus. God's purpose in allowing persecutions, calamity, tribulation and difficulty to come into our lives is so we may take the opportunity to buy gold.

It seems now to me looking back, that God knows how to allow the perfect crisis to hit a person at just the perfect time in order for His perfect will and work to be performed in them. Revelation 3:19 says, "As many as I love, I rebuke and chasten." It is custom made just for you. Our choice was either to give up or buy gold. Yet it seemed to me that the price tag was oh so very high.

Many of these discontents whom we had faithfully counseled and worked with over the years, banked on our character and integrity not to expose them in their ongoing failures and stumblings to the whole congregation. Some of them had had secret affairs on their mates, this fact still unbeknownst to their mates. Others had been involved in deep-seated sins that we had diligently counseled and walked together with them to help them find deliverance and healing.

My vulnerable heart felt like someone had cruelly minced it into a million tiny pieces. These were people I had loved and prayed for daily.

My husband looked like he had been run over by a two ton truck. When Stephen asked Mr. Pride if he could address the congregation, our "spiritual superintendent" told him he was not allowed to speak. Who had ever heard of such a thing, the pastor not being allowed to share his heart with his own congregation?!

I then asked if I could speak. I was granted permission. I stood slowly to my feet and for one long moment just looked people in their faces, eye to eye, looking for some sense of connection with those who were displaying such hate. One by one their eyes dropped to the floor, their shoes somehow becoming vast objects of much needed attention.

I began by asking anyone that I had personally hurt to please forgive me. I suggested that I probably was the cause of much of the discontent and that I was willing to absorb the blame if only we could come to a peaceful resolution.

I then addressed Deacon who was sitting towards the back on the left hand side. I told him that I loved him and his family very much. He sat there looking at me with tears running down his cheeks, shaking his head up and down. I asked him to forgive me of every known and unknown trespass I had ever committed against him. He responded with a nod of his head as he continued to sit there with his head down and cry.

I then went to my seat and sat down. I felt like all the life had been drained from my body. I went into some kind of numb, zombie-like existence through the rest of the meeting. How could life have been so good just a short while ago, and then today, I felt like I was dangling over hell's back door? I truthfully had never felt so badly in my entire life.

The denominational superintendent, with his all knowing spiritual tone, then proceeded to read to the congregation his "supernatural so called God breathed plan" he had received the night before. The sum and whole of it was that Deacon and his cohorts were to be given control of the old facility and the new facility and the pastors, who were dispensable, and all those who were standing with them, were to walk away.

The majority, the people who had stood with the pastors, could not believe their ears! What was he trying to pull?! Then he proceeded to put it to the floor for a vote. He explained the vote in the most confusing way possible, so no one fully understood what they were voting on. He could have spoken to them in another language and they probably would have understood it just as much if not more. Only nasty carnality and the evil demonic powers of hell working together could have come up with such a diabolical plan.

~

WE SINCERELY WANTED A GENUINE RELATIONSHIP WITH GOD MORE THAN ANYTHING ELSE IN LIFE. CLIMBING SOME CORPORATE DENOMINATIONAL LADDER WAS DISTASTEFUL TO US. WE JUST COULDN'T PLAY THE GAME.

~

The votes were taken by ballot, and because of the utter confusion, Superintendent Pride got what he had come gun slinging to town for...the vote his own way that would benefit him and his denomination.

Oh, the divine cave of Adullam God was tailor-making for us! We had heard the promises of God. We had stepped out in faith and in obedience to His Voice, and yet here we were. What were we doing wrong? Where had we missed the leading of the Lord? What were we going to do?

~ PERSONAL REFLECTIONS ~

Does the gold that God challenges us to buy have too high of a price tag on it? Is it better to stay in a neutral, middle of the road status quo and play the political church game?! If this is true, then we were not cut out for the ministry. We sincerely wanted a genuine relationship with God more than anything else in life. Climbing some corporate denominational ladder was distasteful to us. We just couldn't play the game. But yet, our lives probably would have been a lot more peaceful.

Only eternity will tell if the price paid to follow the Lord's will was lived out correctly before Him and our fellow man. The molding process is a tough one, but a necessary one, no matter how God chooses to do it.

THOUGHTS TO PONDER

♦ How does one discern the leading of the Lord from his own defense mechanism?

♦ Why do once strong moves of God, from which denominations have formed, often become organizations of plastic masks and "chosen frozen"?

♦ Discuss how politics infiltrates in among legitimate moves of God.

♦ Is "pure gold" expensive?

♦ Discuss how professionalism is or is not necessarily of God.

♦ Discuss this statement, "Many of these discontents whom we had faithfully counseled and worked with over the years, banked on our character and integrity not to expose them in their ongoing failures and stumblings to the whole congregation."

♦ What is the value in public and private transparency?

SEVEN

~

THE UNEXPECTED
VISITOR

In a moment of time my whole safe, secure, orderly world came suddenly tumbling down around my head. Usually I was a very calm person in the time of crisis or emergency, but because of my great love for this people, it was as though a tremendous evil force had hit my spirit and my emotions head on like a fast moving train coming straight at you. I felt like I couldn't breathe and I needed to get somewhere away from that church where I could get some much needed fresh, cool air into my lungs and clear my fogged out head.

I didn't know where Stephen was, nor could I get my overly stressed brain to try to move my (what felt like two left) feet in the direction he may have been in. All I knew was I had to immediately get out of there. I moved like an over-drugged zombie. My taunt legs and feet were as heavy as lead. I got outside and haphazardly threw my things into our parked car. I should have been going home to relieve the baby sitter, but my tortured mind would not come out of the deep, irky fog it had unexpectedly fallen into.

As I was pulling out of the crowded driveway, Beth one of my faithful youth, now young adult ran up beside the moving car and asked me what I was going to do now. I could only blankly look at her. My mouth would not work. She clung to the side of the car as it was moving, and yelled to me, "You've been the best youth pastor we ever could have had! I don't care what anyone says!"

Her words were echoing in my dizzy head, moving around and around like an out of control merry-go-round. Finally they stopped when I spoke out loud in a whisper to no one in the car, "That's all over with now."

I don't remember driving. All I remember was that I ended up in Howard Johnson's Restaurant, standing in line waiting for a booth. It felt strangely funny to me. Hardly ever did I go out to eat without at least one other person with me, my husband, children or a friend. Here I was all alone, walking in an unfamiliar fog.

~

TO MY STARK AMAZEMENT, I COULDN'T SWALLOW!
THE HOT TEA JUST SWISHED AROUND IN MY
MOUTH. I COULDN'T GET MY THROAT TO WORK!

~

I sat down in the tired looking booth the kind waitress led me to. I didn't even look at the menu. I sensed it would have been a blur before my eyes. The waitress came back to me in a few minutes and asked what I would like. I couldn't get my voice to work. It seemed she sensed as only fellow human beings can, that something was deeply wrong with me. Her tone became even more gentle and patient. She questioned me on a few drinks she could offer and by me nodding my head up and down she came to the conclusion that I could use a cup of tea. She scurried back bringing a little extra pot of hot water along with a worn out looking cup.

I must have poured the water to make tea, because the next thing I consciously remember was trying to swallow. To my stark amazement, I couldn't swallow! The hot tea just swished around in my mouth. I couldn't get my throat to work! I began to panic! I felt the already overly alert muscles in my entire body tighten into what felt like a vise grip. I couldn't get them to relax especially those muscles that usually worked so easily in my throat without me even having to consciously think.

I finally tipped my head back and let it slowly drizzle down the back of my throat. This had never happened to me before! What was going on?!

I don't know how long I sat there, panicked, afraid, alone trying to force back tears that seemed determined to escape from the fixed boundaries of my eyelids. I had never, ever felt like this. As I sat there, I tried to somehow get my twisted mind around what had happened and begin to formulate what we needed to do next. I remember the gold, brownish sweater top and wool skirt I was wearing that night. All I could do was stare at the weave of the cloth of the sweater, as it lay on my arm. My mind was so troubled my eyes seemed to forget how to even blink. It simply refused to work properly.

Somehow I managed to pay my bill and got back into the car. I don't remember driving home. The road and traffic looked all a fuzzy blur. Stephen was beside himself not knowing where I was. He and others had even been out riding the roads looking for me.

I don't remember talking to him or anyone about what had just happened. I was quickly moving towards a complete, dark shutdown. I just couldn't seem to find my way out of this thick, dense, shadowy fog that had completely enveloped around me, sucking me into its seemingly endless vortex.

The next day came. I simply don't remember sleeping or much of anything happening around me. It seems, I do remember, that I was quite concerned for my children, that they were all right and able to get to school, but to get my weighted feet to move or my numb brain to work...no way. It wasn't going to happen.

I locked myself away in our bedroom. I crawled down to the very end of the bed under all of the blankets. I needed to hibernate. My mind needed silence. I couldn't even pray. I couldn't breathe out...even softly the Name of Jesus.

I don't remember how long I stayed in my self-made cocoon, but finally I came out from under the hot covers. Still I couldn't bring myself to comb my hair or do any-thing that was a part of my own daily personal hygiene. I was wrapped in an old white terrycloth bathrobe with a big hole in the side seam. It felt somehow safe and famil-iar. I lived like this for who knows how long, not coming out of that room, not cleaning myself. I couldn't. It was plain and simple. I just couldn't. Something had brutally snapped inside of me and I couldn't fix it.

I would wander into my children's rooms while they were at school and lay on their bedroom floors. Somehow it seemed to comfort me to be near them and their things. I remember sitting on the floor of one of my sons' rooms, my face positioned towards a corner of the room, and rock-ing back and forth pulling my hair. I didn't want my chil-dren to see me like this...yet I wanted and needed to be near them.

I would crawl to the very back of my closet, in my old robe, with my hair snarled and nappy, and just sit there in the dark black of this hidden place, trying to pull my mind and spirit back to some sense of present reality.

As I was in this quiet, dark closet of isolation, one day a knock came on the bedroom door. One of my sons pounded steadily away yelling out, "Obie is here to see you. He has something for you." I hollered back, "Tell him to go away. I can't talk to him right now." I could hear my son's feet racing back down the stairs.

Within a few minutes, I could hear Obie's truck pulling out of the driveway. Soon feet were running back up the stairs and that incessant pounding was heard once again on the door. My son called out, "Mom, you've got to open the door and see this." If it had been anyone else other than one of my children, I wouldn't or should I say I couldn't have opened the door.

Out of the back of that dark closet I slowly crawled, grabbing onto the closet door handle to pull myself up to walk towards the incessant pounding. I little by little opened it, just a crack. My son, seeing the little glimpse of a chance to enter the room, shoved the door wide open and rushed in with the biggest bouquet of flowers I had ever seen. I don't know how much Obie had paid for it, but he must have broken his bank.

You see, Obie was the old patriarch of the O'Brien clan. He had been an alcoholic for a good part of his life. He worked as a stonemason and like the stone he worked with, over time had become hard in his spirit. He'd had a lot of hurt and given out a lot of the same in his life. In the past few years, he had come to the Lord and had made a new beginning to walk with Him. He was never to become a spiritual giant, but he did enter into Jesus' salvation.

Here was this man, who had always been somewhat reclusive and a loner, bringing me this beautiful bouquet of flowers. My son ripped the little card off the bouquet excitedly and thrust it in my face. It read:

God is still in control. He knows what He is doing. Trust Him. Everything is going to work out all right. Love, O'B

I weakly crumbled on the bed with the huge bouquet of flowers leaning over on me. I wept uncontrollably, like a dam had just broken open in me. I don't know how long I lay there with all of this dammed up emotion of festering hurt and whirling confusion rolling out of me just like a raging river. My son stood there for a long while just gently rubbing my back.

All I could wrap myself around was the thought that God had sent Obie O'Brien to me, probably one of the last people I would have thought of that would come to touch my life at its lowest. I knew it was God. Not that Obie was a bad person. No. It was just the fact that he wasn't what we would term a "church person." He wasn't

~

> *ALL I COULD WRAP MYSELF AROUND WAS THE THOUGHT THAT GOD HAD SENT OBIE O'BRIEN TO ME, PROBABLY ONE OF THE LAST PEOPLE I WOULD HAVE THOUGHT OF THAT WOULD COME TO TOUCH MY LIFE AT ITS LOWEST. I KNEW IT WAS GOD.*

~

someone who was "religious," just doing it because he had been taught it was the right thing to do. Obie had been moved by the Spirit of God as a "real person" who had probably been desperately hurting many times in his own life. He came to me based upon a real love and concern from his own heart. He could relate. It wasn't fakey or phony. God knew I couldn't have taken anything like that.

I thank God for using Obie O'Brien, one of the most unlikely people, (but isn't that just like God), to come and touch my life at just that exact moment in time.

From that time on, I was at least able to function. As I began to move, a calm peacefulness fell over me like a warm blanket. I made my way to the shower, washed myself, fixed my hair, brushed my teeth and put on fresh clothes. God had met me.

~ PERSONAL REFLECTIONS ~

God chooses to use unusual people to reach out and touch us. These messengers of God are His choice and how and when is His business also. The mistake we make is expecting God to reach out to us in our own preconceived methods, the way He has touched us in the past. Be assured, He will touch you. God knows and hears your thoughts, even your very sighs. He is a good Father and will not leave you alone without encouraging you in some way. Trust Him…

THOUGHTS TO PONDER

♦ Why is it difficult for a leader to tell someone they need help?

♦ Are there avenues of help for pastors? Are these avenues comfortably approachable and non-judgmental (adding insult to injury) for them? Are they affordable?

♦ Are people idealistic about being in the ministry? Are up and coming leaders trained in the possible hardships they will be called upon to endure?

♦ How can parishioners walk beside leaders and help lift their hands and be an encouragement to them, especially in times of great testing and trial?

EIGHT
~
THE PLOT
THICKENS

Upon the advice of a friend, Stephen began to seek legal counsel. The lawyer suggested we petition for a revote. The members of the leadership who were standing with us, met with everyone possible and signatures were taken. The petition was then presented to the denominational leadership also stating in the petition a request that Head Superintendent Pride, not be allowed to preside over this second congregational meeting.

You would have thought we had shot the Pope! We specifically asked for the assistant superintendent to chair the next congregational meeting. Oh, what a huff when the superintendent walked into the meeting behind his assistant! Superintendent Pride walked down the center aisle seemingly overflowing with arrogance and anger.

Rev. Peacemaker, the assistant superintendent, asked Stephen and Superintendent Pride to come into a room where they could talk privately. The assistant spoke to both men over his understanding that Superintendent Pride had previously falsely accused Stephen of teaching some heretical doctrine to the church. He now was asking him to apologize. The halfhearted apology came slowly.

Stephen then asked his forgiveness for anything he may have done to offend him. Psalm 133:1,2 says "Behold, how good and how pleasant it is for brethren to dwell together in unity! It is like the precious ointment poured on the head, that ran down on the beard, even the beard of Aaron, that came down upon the collar and skirts of his garments (consecrating the whole body)." Stephen was then cautioned to keep the request of Assistant Peacemaker being asked to chair the meeting quiet among the other pastors in the state. They did not want this kind of thing getting out among the brethren. It would have been politically damaging to Superintendent Pride's reputation.

As the people gathered for this strategic meeting, Assistant Superintendent Peacemaker, carefully and fully laid out the details of the revote to the congregation in a very gentle and easy way so that everyone there had a complete understanding of what was being decided.

Before the vote was taken, Rev. Peacemaker asked those who had stirred up such a stink, if they were willing to stay and help maintain a congregation there in the old facility seeing as how they did not want to move on with the present pastor and majority of the members.

Every one of the discontents slowly rose to their feet. Oh, how obstinately prideful they held their heads, faces twisted in total defiance. Many of their expressions reminded me of spoiled, rebellious children throwing a fitful temper tantrum.

Both Rev. Peacemaker and Rev. Pride stressed the importance to them of sticking with this work and not abandoning it later on down the road. All those standing, nodded their heads vigorously in assent that they were fully and truly committed to staying and making it work. They emanated a religious attitude of "You can count on us! We'll be true blue."

Deacon rose in an infuriated sulk, heat steaming off his face, and stated that if the vote was overturned, he was going to bring heavy lawsuits and liens fast and furious against those who wanted to move on and finish the new sanctuary. He heatedly threatened that we had no concept of what he could do to us.

Previously, he had threatened Stephen and other board members in a board meeting that he could "buy them all at one end of the street and sell them at the other." He went around the table in one heated meeting and individually pointed to each board member and told them as he pointed at each one in a red-faced, infuriated rage, "I can destroy you. I can destroy you. And I can destroy you." In days to come not one of them who took a stand would be left out from feeling the weight of his intimidating words. He was not making idle threats in the board meeting or in the congregational meeting. He intended to do just what he promised.

One board member, Carl, came to us later and told us prior to this second congregational meeting that Deacon had come to him while he was working on the new sanctuary. He handed him a check for twenty-five thousand dollars from the church building fund telling him to begin working on building himself a new house. This was the man who had sold his house previously and had given fifty thousand dollars into the building fund. He was taken back, knowing that no amount of money greater than five thousand dollars could be spent without congregational approval, yet here Deacon was offering this enormous figure to him.

It was easy for Deacon to move church funds around as his wife was the present treasurer of the church. She was a precious woman, gentle and sweet. He, at times, could be full of fun and loving the Lord and then at the next moment be in a horrible, angry temper over something no one else understood or knew about. She always stood with him and as a good wife, tried to obey and work with him. For Deacon to get a check written for five thousand dollars without any of the other board members or pastor having knowledge of it, was not hard.

Deacon asked to meet with Carl. Upon handing the check to Carl, he stated that another five thousand dollars would be forthcoming. Carl's heart sank when he saw the church building fund name on the check and the realization dawned on him that Deacon was using church money to try and buy his support.

Thank God for this dear brother's integrity and character before God and man. Carl reported his news immediately to Stephen and the check was given to Brown, our newly appointed treasurer. A new account was opened with this five thousand dollars check. That money was to become the money that would support us in those first few difficult months after the revote and move.

Also within this time period, Carl was taken to a nearby city by Deacon and shown a vacant commercial building. Deacon told him that he would set up a church, all expenses paid for him to come and pastor. Oh, what a wilderness temptation for him! Deacon was trying to use this as another tool to get him to switch his loyalty to him from the pastor and the vision of God burning in his own heart. Carl later became an assistant pastor to the work going forward and still holds this position until this present time.

Who could believe that this noxious evil had burst out all around us? How were we to know that we were just in the beginning throws of our journey of the dark night of our soul?

The long awaited vote was taken by Assistant Superintendent Peacemaker. Oh, what tension there was in that place! You could hear people mouthing things sarcastically under their breath. The air seemed charged with demonic scurrying and lucid, hellish activity. All I wanted to do was have this over and done with...whatever way it came out.

~

I SAT THERE THINKING WHAT HAD WE COME TO THAT PEOPLE WERE BECOMING PHYSICALLY ILL IN THE HOUSE OF GOD? THIS SHOULD BE A PLACE OF HEALING AND WHOLENESS AND LOVING RESTORATION...YET HERE WE WERE IN THIS VIPEROUS, STEALTHY HOLE TRYING TO JUST SURVIVE.

~

The counters collected the votes, sitting on the front row where the superintendents could watch carefully as every vote was counted and tallied. The room became increasingly quiet. I could hear my own stomach growl with nervousness. One of the dear women sitting in front of me had developed an upset stomach under the weighty stress of it all. She tried discreetly to get to the restroom without being sick all over the floor.

I sat there thinking what had we come to that people were becoming physically ill in the house of God? This should be a place of healing and wholeness and loving restoration...yet here we were in this viperous, stealthy hole trying to just survive.

The Assistant Superintendent pushed his chair back from the table that had been placed on the platform. He stood with a piece of paper in his hand with the results of the vote. You couldn't hear even a breath being breathed in or out. Oh, the tension!

He took a deep breath himself, almost seeming not to want to have to give the results, knowing that one side was not going to be happy and he would be the one to feel the first blow of their rage. Out came his breath and with it the results.

The old church facility was to be deeded to those who had stood and committed themselves to it. The new facility was to be finished by those who wanted to go on with the pastor.

A loud, victorious cheer went up from the greater majority, those who had been fasting and praying for victory over this horrendous catastrophe. The Lord had prevailed! On the other hand, oh, the ugly comments spewing out of uncontrolled, fuming lips. It was so painfully hurtful to my spirit and deeply wounded and grieved me. What were their thoughtless words doing to the heart of the Lord?

A dear brother in the church asked if he could address the people. Luke had been the boys' club leader for many years, even long before we had come to pastor this congregation. He spoke out, "You all know how much I love the boys of this congregation. I would like to leave the denominational charter for our club with this present group so they will not have to form a new club. I'm giving this only on the promise that someone will carry on the work with the boys who will be staying." He then handed the charter to one of the people who had stood, and went and sat down.

A notary of the public had been asked to be present at the meeting. The plan had been that if the vote was reversed that the old facility would be deeded to those staying for one dollar. The paper work was drawn up and the needed signatures made. We were now entering into the next leg of the journey of the dark night of our souls.

~ PERSONAL REFLECTIONS ~

"What fellowship has darkness with light?" This is the question God's Word asks us. Darkness can come dressed up in a nice suit, white shirt and tie, spewing out religious talk, but only having a form of godliness, denying the power thereof to allow the Spirit of God into the inner chambers of the heart to do the deeper work only He knows how to do. Young, naïve soldiers of the cross often think that this level of darkness cannot and will not be within their particular ranks. Wake up! We all are flesh and blood susceptible to the weaknesses of our own flesh and reasoning.

We had worshipped and fellowshipped with Deacon for nine years. We had never applied a sense of caution with him or anyone else in all our lives. We needed to have heeded the old saying, "Beware when all men speak well of you," over the years. If things seem to be too good to be true, they usually are. Our previous growth was great. We should have been aware the enemy of our souls would react to it. And he would use those you thought you could have most relied on to stand with you.

THOUGHTS TO PONDER

♦ How do you dissect politics from denominationalism and the path God would have for a body of people?

♦ Are halfhearted apologies true healing apologies that work on a true spiritual level?

♦ Is control and manipulation ever profitable in the Kingdom of God? Can this be disguised, ambushing people into thinking what it is working is the will of God? What are our safeguards against this?

♦ Did Carl do the right thing? Was God testing his loyalty to his pastor and to God Himself?

Hell tipped its head forward to listen and watch that night of the revote with bated breath. I can just see the demons assigned to us wringing their hands with anticipation over our defeat! Sorry!! No goal! God had diverted their plan and had given us just enough hope and leverage to survive. "The Lord knows the way that I take. When He has tried me I shall come forth as pure gold." The "trying" part isn't fun. It never is. But it is necessary in the eyes of God. He did not even spare His own Son from this. Know He knows the way you also take. He knows how to bring you through...not bypass around, but through.

♦ Does demonic activity enter in to a foray such as this? When and where did it get access?

♦ How do such experiences affect people for the rest of their lives?

♦ Where could this body of people have reached out for help and guidance other than the denomination they had naively and blindly been a part of? Were they ready to willingly trust anyone, especially someone not known to them?

NINE

~

SET YOUR FACE
LIKE A FLINT

When the tumultuous volcano had erupted and continued to flow dangerously hot, the pressure that came upon us was like nothing I had ever known or experienced before in my entire life. When you thought it could never get worse, it would. My first immediate reaction had been that we should leave...the sooner the better. This was not how it was with Stephen. He wanted to stay and see this thing through. There was absolutely nothing within me, no hidden inner reservoir within to muster up the courage to match his at this time. Everything looked bleakly hopeless to me. The only light I saw at the end of the tunnel looked to me just like a fast moving train headed straight for us.

Stephen would try to convince me that God was in this somewhere and that He was still in control, yet no amount of talking would solidly convince me enough to change my mind. I wanted to leave without delay. Living under this pounding pressure was like sitting in a dentist's chair having a root canal. The dentist leaves halfway through the procedure, the anesthesia wears off and you can't get up and leave nor can you stand the constant, intense pain. You're trapped! The dentist doesn't come back and your poor tooth is exposed to cold air and you're seeking tongue keeps poking the open cavern as it is only trying to figure out what to do to help relieve the pain of its neighbor. What a dilemma, yet that was how I felt, to put it mildly.

During one of our frequent midnight discussions we agreed that we would fast and pray for three days. We also agreed together that we would not talk with anyone, including each other over what the Lord would say to us during the three days. In Luke 2:37 and Acts 13:3 it tells us that before major decisions were made, they took time to seek the Lord through fasting and prayer. When we fast, we are saying that we are totally focused and dependent on God, because we understand no one else, except God, can give us the answers that we truly need.

~

WHEN WE FAST, WE ARE SAYING THAT WE ARE TO-TALLY FOCUSED AND DEPENDENT ON GOD, BECAUSE WE UNDERSTAND NO ONE ELSE, EXCEPT GOD, CAN GIVE US THE ANSWERS THAT WE TRULY NEED.

~

We both were good to our word as we desperately needed to hear the direction the Lord would have us take. We both desired to stay in the center of God's will, even if it meant some more hard times…then so be it. We wanted Him to speak very clearly to us, to rid us of powerful doubts that would surely come to haunt us later on down the road.

At the end of the three day period, we met together to share from our hearts what the Lord had spoken to us. I was apprehensively nervous. I suggested to Stephen that he go first, hoping that what he had received from the Lord would be different from me.

He started out slowly, building momentum as only he can in telling a tale. My heart stopped beating. I couldn't believe what I was hearing! It was the same exact passage of Scripture I had received! I stopped him halfway through his telling. This was so amazing! It had to be the Lord speaking this clearly to us. I was ecstatic that He was speaking so plainly, yet I did not like what He was saying.

Both of us had gotten Ezekiel 3:8, 9. It reads like this: "Behold, I have made your face strong against their faces, and your forehead strong against their foreheads. Like adamant stone, harder than flint, I have made your forehead; do not be afraid of them, nor be dismayed at their looks, though they are a rebellious house."

We both were glad for the supernatural answer we had received. We both truly wanted only what God wanted, yet we could only guess at the costly price He would require us to pay in the months and years to come.

I wonder today if we had known then what we know now, would we have continued on the journey of the dark night of our souls.

~ PERSONAL REFLECTIONS ~

To prepare some of His servants, God strategically imprisons them. The apostle Paul was imprisoned by God, and in his case it was a literal prison. He, too, had to set his face like a flint in order not to give in to despair. Never once did he say, "I'm a Roman prisoner." In his letter to the Ephesians, he used three phrases to describe himself: "I, Paul, the prisoner of Christ Jesus" (3:1); "the prisoner of the Lord" (4:1); "I am an ambassador in chains" (6:20). Paul thoroughly understood that even though the Romans had arrested him, it was God who had planned his imprisonment, and as such he insisted that he was God's prisoner.

The Word of the Lord to us which we had received through fasting and prayer was hard to receive, yet we knew it was from God. He wanted us to yield to His plan. He was looking for complete obedience. He was bringing us into a place of limitation and restriction with a companionship of absolute helplessness to change anything, and no divine mandate to initiate change.

~

HE WAS BRINGING US INTO A PLACE OF LIMITATION AND RESTRICTION WITH A COMPANIONSHIP OF ABSOLUTE HELPLESSNESS TO CHANGE ANYTHING, AND NO DIVINE MANDATE TO INITIATE CHANGE.

~

We were imprisoned by circumstances and by financial constraints. Although we did not feel the real iron shackles on us, nevertheless they were just as real. We were with Job when he cried out, "Why is light given to a man whose way is hidden, and whom God has hedged in?" Job 3:23. Lamentations 3:7-9 says, "He has hedged me in so that I cannot get out; He has made my chain heavy. Even when I cry and shout, He shuts out my prayer. He has blocked my ways with hewn stone; He has made my paths crooked." How long oh Lord was this to continue? Only God knew. I was to learn later that God was using this particular season of imprisonment to mature the wine of our love and to get us ready for greater fruitfulness. We just needed to hang on.

THOUGHTS TO PONDER

♦ What part does fasting play in our search for answers from God? Can certain answers be found outside of fasting and prayer?

♦ What is it like when God gives such specific instruction—given in great clarity?

♦ Is there a danger in not following His direction?

♦ How could this word, "set your face like a flint" be an encouragement and then again be a discouragement? ·

TEN

~

STRUCK DOWN, BUT NOT OUT

The next few weeks were hellish to say the least. I couldn't bring myself to go back into that building for services. Stephen went through the motions of leading the worship services under extreme stressful pressure. I was not spiritually or emotionally mature enough at the time to understand that I should have embraced the pain. God didn't want me to waste my pain but use it. He was trying to encourage me to allow it to do its work of purging, purifying and strengthening.

Betrayal is not good; it is not from God. But I needed to embrace the pain so that it could do some positive things in me. It is like an athlete who embraces and endures pain. It eventually will produce good. I often think of Moses and his staff. In the Hebrew, the word for staff is **matteh** which means scepter, staff – representing brokenness, meekness and confidence in God alone. Moses judged nations, parted seas, brought forth water from a rock and held his staff high on a mountaintop which caused victory over the enemies of God. This staff was not a staff representing Moses' strength but one that represented his weakness. Brokenness allows God to place His authority in us.

God was trying to groom us so that He could place a staff in our hands. He was trying to teach us that He places this staff in our hands at the very place of brokenness. We **must** be broken and poured out. The full anointing God would use to flow through us cannot be released until this process of brokenness happens.

~

GOD WAS TRYING TO GROOM US SO THAT HE COULD PLACE A STAFF IN OUR HANDS. HE WAS TRYING TO TEACH US THAT HE PLACES THIS STAFF IN OUR HANDS AT THE VERY PLACE OF BROKENNESS.

~

After several Sundays of going through the motions of having church in the old facility, we found a large enough place in a motel not far from the new building. There was a sense of great relief not having to be under that dark cloud of tense dissension, yet we felt a little like fish out of water, never before having to set up for a worship service in a motel.

Even though there was a sense of relief, you could still feel under the surface in many people, a seething anger and bleeding hurt. Your mind wanted to race ahead and talk about normal things like the weather and Christmas, only we all were obsessively preoccupied with all that had happened to us that had been out of our control.

The tone of the service was one of relief heavily coated with fresh, bleeding sorrow. God is never pleased when brethren cannot dwell in unity together...unless they can walk away with a right spirit to "agree to disagree" and still walk in the love of the Lord. None of us had made it that far. God had plans for us though.

Somehow, unwisely, we all felt that the children could continue on in the same school together, using the old facility to house the school. You would have thought we all had taken classes in "How to be Dumb 101." Of course if parents are angry and wounded, wouldn't this attitude and hurt be passed on to teachers and students? We soon found out just how true this was.

The majority of the students were children whose parents were standing with the pastor. Eventually another church offered their facility to us, to move our portion of the school into their building through the rest of the school year. We accepted their offer. We were most thankful for their outstretched hand of helpful friendship. We had been through so much; we were beginning to wonder if every door in life was going to be a closed one.

Gradually we began to take on a "leper mentality," at least I did. I remember being in the supermarket, looking at a stranger, wondering if they knew what a failure I was. Somehow, I felt everyone in the community knew every detail of all that had happened. I realize now, between myself and the voice of the enemy I was being hoodwinked, but I didn't realize this all back then.

I would purposely hold my head down, my eyes cast to the floor, whenever I was in public. I was ashamed and confused in my mind and spirit. I wanted people to see Jesus when they looked at me, not a broken weary person, yet that is exactly what I was and probably exactly what they saw.

The following year, we moved our school into the homes of the teachers. I taught eight children in my home for that year. It was a challenge to home school that many, mostly high school and two of my own children who were younger. Now I look back and realize God was creating a shelter for these precious students (who had been wounded on their own level and understanding) and me where we could have great times of fellowship and camaraderie together. Yes, we had to revamp alot of classes like gym, etc., yet God was using this time to heal and restore my spirit to health. God allowed humorous things to happen and through the laughter, healing began to flow like a strong medicine against the continuous bleeding pain of the past.

Deacon sent flatbed trucks to the uncompleted church, backed up to the doors and took truckloads of building materials out of the building. Around that same time, he began to send developers to come and walk through the building with them repeating to us that he was going to sell the building. Needless to say, all the locks were quickly changed.

The project was grinding to a complete halt. Oh, the tension in the air. Stephen and Carl trying to still push the construction forward under these almost impossible circumstances, were filled with sorrow, yet still having small embers of faith flickering in them. Before leaving the building on one of these hard days, Carl stayed and put up an oak cross in the back of the sanctuary between two walls under construction, and declared that this would be God's church and He would have the say. This was truly an act of blind faith because there wasn't one positive thing happening that you could have hung your hat on.

December was not to be as pleasant a month as it usually was for us. Our services in the motel were only on Sunday afternoons as other churches and meetings filled the motel's rooms at other possible times. No other place was available.

~

WORSHIP THAT MINISTERED TO HIS SPIRIT WAS DONE IN SPIRIT AND IN TRUTH, OUT OF A VESSEL THAT WAS BROKEN AND HUMBLED BEFORE HIM.

~

Nothing was as we had planned or thought it would be. Our church nursery was now a motel room. Children's church was held in another little off room usually used for executive board meetings. A portable keyboard had to be set up and a little speaker and mike found. Life had truly changed in a moment. Sad to say, that even the portable keyboard was to meet a final death blow when it got left in a hot car, with the sun beating down on it melting its major components. It could not be fixed. I felt like I was being stripped of every possible thing, even the instrument I used to help lead us into worship was taken from me. I am not a proficient guitarist, but that was what we were forced to resort to to have any music at all to help lead the congregation along. What a step backwards for me from a beautiful grand piano to a simple strumming away on my guitar. God was trying to teach me that true heart-felt worship which touched and pleased His heart was not necessarily going to happen because of my gifting to play a magnificent piano. Worship that ministered to His Spirit was done in spirit and in truth, out of a vessel that was broken and humbled before Him. What a far cry from many worship services I had personally led His people into over the years I had been a worship leader sitting at a baby grand.

By January, all hired staff had to come off salary, including my husband. Stephen took a precarious job cutting wood for another man in the church. This isn't a particularly good time of the year to be out doing this sort of work in sub-zero weather, yet he did it with a willing heart. I know it was very hard for him, and I'm sure he wondered many times what God was doing.

Numerous days Stephen had to dangle himself over the side of a hill by a sturdy rope and work all day with a cumbersome chain saw, cutting trees down, in bitter cold weather to put food on our table. I'll always admire and thank him for being the man he had to be for the welfare of his children and myself. Our children never realized that we were going through some of the hardest financial times of our lives because of their father's character and heart before them and God. Single ladies, don't ever settle for anyone less than a real man of God, or you, somewhere in life will be sorely disappointed and grievously wounded. God was using this cold, lonely hillside to teach my husband deeper character lessons than he ever thought he would have to learn. Oh how God can strip us and take us back to the basics to learn yet once again, the things that really matter in life.

Work still went on to finish the new facility with all of us pecking away at whatever little jobs we could find to do. People came in the evenings and on Saturdays, as much as possible to try and finish this project. Materials were nil if next to nothing. We took what little funds we had to buy materials to keep making some progress. We were determined to keep going forward.

One day in February, an official legal server came to the church to serve us with a mechanic lien from one of Deacon's companies. This scene was to play itself out over and over again, with many such liens and lawsuits, each time no less painful than the first. I would get this sick all over feeling, and my heart would pound out of rhythm at the nerve wracking news. It is no easy thing having liens and lawsuits, one after another served on you, especially when they are threatening to tear the very vision of God out of your heart.

Deacon was very good at psychologically playing with our minds. We had never swum in these deep waters. He was coming good on his past threats and was comfortable dealing in this "dog eat dog" arena. We were novices, with no money to work with and no experience on how to survive.

At the same time, the denomination we had been with faithfully for thirteen years decided that we were not co-operating with them to their satisfaction. They were making plans to move in on us and take the new facility away from the congregation.

In order to leave this particular denomination, you had to have one hundred percent of the congregational vote to walk. If just one person decides they want to stay with that denomination, that's how it will go. You have to then hand the key over to them and walk away. This is never brought to your attention upon entering this denomination. Easy to get in, hard to get out, like the cockroach motel.

At this time a request from the congregation was made that I be installed as co-pastor to serve along side my husband. I had always been content to minister as the youth pastor; in fact I think my heart will always be inclined towards that age group. They have so much potential in the Lord. And they always love to have fun. The congregation continued to press this issue, and I was installed as co-pastor.

~ PERSONAL REFLECTIONS ~

I have often wondered if it is in the omniscient plan of God that every child of His goes through some seasons of being broken. Somehow in theory, it would seem fair and right if everyone had to, but it appears not to be the case. Moses, David, Joseph, and Paul, to name a few, but then there were those you never read of going through this depth of brokenness. What would be the survey today for the Christian walking with God? Does He tailor make our valleys to groom us for our futures? Does He **have** to bring us to rock bottom lows?

My heart goes out to you if you are walking through just that kind of valley at this moment. Don't take on a leper mentality such as I did. Listen to one who has walked there before you—you are called and ordained by God. He has hand-picked you for a greater purpose whether you will be known by man or not, your name will be known where it really counts...in heaven. Hold your head up high and repeat to yourself, "This world is not my home. I'm

~

DON'T TAKE ON A LEPER MENTALITY SUCH AS I DID. LISTEN TO ONE WHO HAS WALKED THERE BEFORE YOU—YOU ARE CALLED AND ORDAINED BY GOD.

~

just passing through." And pass through with a heavenly dignity whether you understand all God is working in and around you today or not. Know that He is a wonderful Father and knows exactly what He is doing. He said He would turn everything for good if we are called according to His purpose, and you are. Snuff out the voicesof doubt and depression. Get a song in your heart and tune in to the heavenly station...channel 777 in the heavenly realm. I'm sure you'll like what you hear.

THOUGHTS TO PONDER

♦ Do you think everyone has to go through seasons of brokenness or just those called to greater levels of responsibility?

♦ Why does God sometimes take away every tool and prop you are used to leaning on?

♦ Do you think some miss their times of blessing and harvest because they are not willing to walk through the valleys and times of leanness?

♦ Godly character is needed not just in times of temptation but also in times of hardship. What is to gain or lose by this?

♦ What is a "leper mentality"? How do you get past it?

♦ What fears come when leaving familiar denominational frameworks?

ELEVEN

~

WHEN THE LIGHTS GO OUT

"For You will light my lamp; the LORD my God will enlighten my darkness." (Psalm 18:28).

Never had we been in such a treacherous position! God was allowing this crisis to come our way for the purpose of maturing and forming godly character in us. Our response in the middle of all of this was, "Lord, why is this happening to us?" We didn't understand what God was doing, and as much as we sought Him about it, the heavens seemed to be like brass. Why wouldn't God talk to us right then about it?

God allows this darkness for some of His servants to walk through. Isaiah 50:10-11 says, "Who is among you who fears the Lord, who obeys the voice of His Servant, yet who walks in darkness and deep trouble and has no shining splendor in his heart? Let him rely on, trust in, and be confident in the Name of the Lord, and let him lean upon and be supported by his God. Behold, all you (enemies of your own selves) who attempt to kindle your own fires (and work out your own plans of salvation), who surround and gird yourselves with momentary sparks, darts, and firebrands that you set aflame!-walk by the light of your self-made fire and of the sparks that you have kindled (for yourself, if you will)! But this shall you have from My hand; you shall lie down in grief and in torment." I would like to share some thoughts regarding the dark valley season we were walking through, God's purposes in it, and how He led us out.

David wrote in Psalm 23:4, "Yea, though I walk through the valley of the shadow of death, I will fear no evil; for You are with me." David knew what it was like to walk through dark seasons when you don't know what God is doing, where He seems to have gone and you can't see beyond your own nose. Looking back, I understand now that He was refining us in this dark valley and then bringing us out into the sunshine of His maturity and fruitfulness. God's purpose is to help us to walk **through** the valley.

~

GOD'S PURPOSE IS TO HELP US TO WALK THROUGH THE VALLEY.

~

During this dark season, we felt like we were under total immersion by this overwhelming deluge of fiery trial. We had to quickly decide if we were going to try to push our way out of the valley in our own strength and reasoning or yield ourselves, by faith, to let God help us grow out of the valley. The only way to survive was to seek the Lord passionately and continuously. By making our way along in this manner, God's grace was released to us in measure to help our feet touch bottom enough not to sink and to help our spiritual legs go downwards, planting our roots into the soil of this unknown valley.

Isaiah 40:3-4 says "The voice of one crying in the wilderness: "Prepare the way of the Lord; make straight in the desert a highway for our God. Every valley shall be exalted and every mountain and hill brought low; the crooked places shall be made straight and the rough places smooth." The purpose in this valley experience was the making of a highway in our hearts for God. On this highway, God was going to lead us out of the valley we were in.

This highway is built by "every valley being exalted." Our first instinct was to try as hard as we could to get ourselves out of this horrible trial. It was a long, unhappy season, a time I wished then, could have been totally avoided. I wanted out of this dark place as soon as possible. But the Lord exalts those who let the fullness of the valley season work in their lives. Luke 3:4 says it this way, "Every valley shall be filled." Jesus promises us, at these times and seasons of our lives, that He will fill us with a fresh fullness of His Spirit and exalt us to a higher plane of maturity in Him.

"And every mountain and hill brought low" – Through no fault of our own, but through circumstances totally outside of our control, we were brought down. There was no scandal or moral failure. God's purpose was to be introduced in this valley season, in order that we would learn the truest ways of God.

"The crooked places shall be made straight" – These are areas and understanding in our lives where we think we are actually pretty straight, when in the eyes of God, we are not. The Lord will take great care to straighten out what we have not even thought to question.

"And the rough places smooth" – Our personalities and characters, our personal qualities and attributes that were unknowingly abrasive and counterproductive to God's kingdom were in for a bit of a sanding. We could not see these things as He could and were totally incapable of helping ourselves. In His mercy, God brought others into our lives that were used as iron to sharpen iron. The only stones that will make a mark in any giant's head are smooth ones.

One of the reasons we are unable to hear from God

when the darkness of the valley experience encompasses us like a flood, is that God wants to "re-teach" the way in which we listen to Him. Psalm 23:4 says, "Yea, though I walk through the valley of the shadow of death, I will fear no evil; for You are with me; Your rod and Your staff, they comfort me." In this place in the valley, it was hard for me at first to know whether I was hearing God accurately, and because I wanted to hear His Voice so much, I would strain my ears trying to hear Him. Looking back now, I understand that was exactly what He wanted. When a sheep is following his shepherd on a normal day, he will use both sight and sound – seeing where he is going. He follows the shepherd's voice and also the sound of his feet. But when a sheep is left out in the darkness, when the sheep can't see where the shepherd is going, he has to totally rely on his sense of hearing. One of the things a sheep will strain to hear is his shepherd's staff. This staff is used as a walking stick, and the shepherd will tap it on the ground or rocks which will help the sheep know where the shepherd is going. The sheep is guided by his sense of hearing.

The Lord was teaching us not to go as we had done for so many years, on what we could see He was doing spiritually. In fact, during this valley season, if we had gone by what we saw, we would have curled up in a ball and died. It was only by learning to passionately seek Him and learning to really **listen** to His Voice that we survived. This season was a major class on learning how to cultivate our spiritual ears. There is nothing wrong with seeing things in the Spirit, but there is more to the supernatural realm than what can be discerned with our spiritual eyes.

Our spiritual ears were learning to pick up spiritual realities that we were not able to perceive with our spiritual seeing. Romans 4:7 says that "God calls things that are not as though they were." The spiritual eye sees nothing, but the spiritual ear hears the Voice of God calling it into being.

In John 10:27 Jesus said "My sheep hear My voice, and I know them, and they follow Me." This is how Jesus guided us through this dark valley. He wants us to be guided by our sense of spiritual hearing as well as spiritual sight.

~

TAKE NOTE WHEN YOU ARE IN THE DARK;
HE IS GOING TO SPEAK TO YOU. AND WHAT HE
SPEAKS TO YOU, YOU WILL DECLARE WHEN
YOUR DARK NIGHT HAS PASSED.

~

It seemed many times that God was not speaking, when we would begin to look back and realize He actually had spoken a lot of things to us. We began to write this all down and discuss and pray about these things together. He didn't necessarily talk to us alot about the actual darkness, (which of course was what we wanted Him to talk to us about), but He was speaking many other things into our hearts. Jesus talked about this in Matthew 10:27. He said, "Whatever I tell you in the dark, speak in the light." Take note when you are in the dark; He is going to speak to you. And what He speaks to you, you will declare when your dark night has passed.

THOUGHTS TO PONDER

♦ Do you truly believe God allows crisis to come our way for the purpose of maturing and forming godly character in us?

♦ Have there been times that you have run from the valley experience rather than letting it have its perfect work?

♦ What do you think of the statement, "The only stones that will make a mark in any giant's head are smooth ones." What does this mean?

♦ Discuss the importance of learning to hear in the dark and not always having to "see" what God is working.

TWELVE
~
SWIMMING WITH
THE SHARKS

The pressure of having multitudinous liens put on us was nearly unbearable. We had no idea how to protect ourselves as a church, nor the funds wherewith to do it.

When the church had agreed with Deacon to take on a two hundred thousand dollar bullet loan early on in the beginning of the project, he convinced us there would be no problem for us to pay this money back within the one year period. He gave his word, (I know, I know), that it would be taken care of. If we had only known then what we know now...

Here we were, fast approaching the deadline when this money would have to be repaid. Deacon knew that if we couldn't come up with it, it was all over. He would take everything—the building, the land, everything we had invested in with our money, time and hard work, that is, after he probably had fought it out with the denomination he was still a part of.

We were counseled by those who had some knowledge of this kind of battle, to hire a good lawyer. Stephen and I had never had any experience in dealing with lawyers previous to this. Stephen began to seek out advice from those who had as to whom would do a good job for us, and one name kept surfacing. We went to him and laid our story out on the table. This man decided he would take our case. Thus began the journey of indebtedness to our lawyers at the tune of one hundred twenty five to one hundred fifty dollars an hour. Oh, what joy!

In the back of our minds, we knew we had to fight, but there was this constant, irritating, nagging voice persistently asking this one simple question. Where were we going to get the money to pay them off when the time came?!

On top of all of this, our corporate lawyer counseled us that we needed to hire a bankruptcy lawyer as well. More pure joy! What wondrous news. Could life get any better?! One was found that would work for us at the same tune as the first lawyer. Now we would be paying double on the hour for their combined expertise. As my husband so aptly would describe this season in our lives, "We were learning to swim with the sharks!" Oh, how right he was!

∼

DON'T EVER BE CARELESS OVER THE PAPER WORK OF YOUR MINISTRY!

∼

The lawyers began by having us go back through all of the books of the church. We had to look for discrepancies in money coming in and money going out. This would help us to get a firm footing. The only trouble was, Deacon and his wife would not turn over the church books. Remember, she had been the treasurer for several years. So thus began a tug of war to get these documents. Our church legally owned all the books, records, and other corporate paperwork of the church from the past up to the present. Our lawyers finally had to take legal action to get them released into our hands.

When these documents and books did arrive, we had to go over them with a fine tooth comb. Some things were missing and some things looked like they had been changed.

The paper trail was a maze of tracks first leading here, then there, not easy to follow.

The lawyers wanted everything scanned from years back up to the present. Every check had to be put in order according to number. Every board meeting and congregational meeting had to be examined to study the exact wording of each and every statement and vote.

Don't ever be careless over the paper work of your ministry! Always keep a clear paper trail! It could someday save the life of your church or outreach. Be meticulous over every detail. Many times I have thanked God for the careful scrutiny my husband has had over this area of the church and our own affairs. If he had not done so, we never would have survived.

A judge will always want to see the "paper trail" in any case of any kind. He will not just take your word for it. He needs to see the documentation of every jot and tittle. Whether seemingly unimportant at the time or not, keep good accounts and records. It really does matter! I Corinthians 4:2 tells us "Moreover, it is (essentially) required of stewards that a man should be found faithful (proving himself worthy of trust)." Every penny and every piece of paper matters. Every invoice and receipt matters when it comes to the things of the house of the Lord.

Soon cardboard boxes of documentation began to accumulate. Every bit had some significance. These boxes had to be kept in a secure place, under lock and key, where no one else but those who had authority could work with them.

Banks had to be contacted as there were missing checks that had been cashed, yet had not been put in with other returned church checks. We began putting every last detail of every last report and every last check and every last vote in order from the time we had come to the present.

So began my seemingly endless nights of typing and retyping. Every portion of information that we thought may have significance, needed a supporting explanation from Stephen so the lawyers would be very clear on how everything fit in and tied together.

While we worked without stopping on all of this, finding out what was missing, putting the remaining evidence in order, etc., we knew that the deadline for the two hundred thousand dollar bullet loan was just around the corner. Our lawyers told us if we could not come up with the money, we should file Chapter 11. Chapter 11 is not bankruptcy. In Chapter 11 you are given time to reorganize your corporation. It doesn't mean you can't pay your bills. It means it looks like you may be able to and you are given time to convince the court that you can by coming up with a doable plan to show you are able to generate the funds needed to stay in business and pay off your debts.

So began the all-nighters brainstorming what we could do and how this could be put down on paper to be presented to the judge.

Then came another blow. Not only were these bogus liens of almost a million dollars staring us in the face, at this time the lawyers told us we needed $5000 to file for Chapter 11. We were to learn that anything to do with the courts and with lawyers will cost you astronomical fees which seemingly never end, but just keep coming.

We, as a church, began to fast and pray asking the Lord to release $5000 for this filing. Retainers of large sums of money (to us), had to be given to our lawyers up front. We had all, every one of us, sacrificed everything we had to hire them. It was a matter of life and death for our church existence and God had begun with His own house first. He had asked us to give sacrificially, everything possible, until we had all given out everything that we possibly had to give. With all of this added expense, we were just barely able to keep the rental costs for the motel rooms to meet on Sundays paid.

Stephen had come off salary as had everyone else. We, as a family, had pledged at the beginning of the building project, to pay double tithes until the building was completely finished. We never could have guessed the length of time this would have taken, yet we agreed we were not going to break our commitment that had been made in sincerity before the Lord. God was testing our obedience and trust in His provision.

Others who had been on staff had taken jobs with the local city hospital. Some of us were teaching in our homes. Others were working in a stone quarry. We all were doing what we had to to get by. There just was no extra money among us for this emergency.

~

GOD WAS TESTING OUR OBEDIENCE AND TRUST IN HIS PROVISION.

~

As the time drew near, Stephen called everyone he could think of, from one coast to the other, asking for a loan for just a short period of time. The well seemed dry. No one we knew was in a position to help us.

The night before the deadline of the dreaded morning felt like we were trapped in a very long, tedious nightmare. We both were up through the entire night pacing the floor in intercessory prayer. Was this the beginning of the end for us? Neither one of us had much to say...you know, that kind of time when you just don't know what to say.

Oh, how dark our world seemed that night! The constant ticking of the clock and the hum of the refrigerator seemed maddeningly loud. Would we ever reach the dawn of the morning? Yet we really didn't want it to come...answerless. What deep, fathomless darkness your journey can take you on through the dark night of your soul. Was God still in this?! Or was He busy working on the other side of the earth?

There wasn't a single thing more we could do. Not one. We had fasted. We had prayed. We had asked friends and loved ones for their help. Nothing but a big, fat zero.

It was all up to God if we were to survive. We were like Elijah at the brook Cherith. I Kings 17:5-7 says "So he (Elijah) did according to the word of the Lord; he went and dwelt by the brook Cherith, east of the Jordan. And the ravens brought him bread and flesh in the morning and bread and flesh in the evening, and he drank of the brook. After a while the brook dried up because there was no rain in the land."

~

OUR EYES WERE FIRMLY FIXED ON THE LORD. WE HAD NO STRENGTH OR WHERE-WITH-ALL TO HELP OURSELVES. IT WAS TIME TO EITHER SINK OR SWIM.

~

We were truly shut up to Him. In our deep darkness, all we could do was stand still now and lean totally upon the Name of our God. We knew better than to try and create something out of our own thinking that was not from the Lord. Isaiah 50:11 says, "Behold, all you (enemies of your own selves) who attempt to kindle your own fires (and work out your own plans of salvation), who surround and gird yourselves with momentary sparks, darts, and firebrands that you set aflame!-walk by the light of your self-made fire and of the sparks that you have kindled (for yourself, if you will)! But this shall you have from My hand: you shall lie down in grief and in torment." Our eyes were firmly fixed on the Lord. We had no strength or where-with-all to help ourselves. It was time to either sink or swim. The choice was definitely God's and not ours.

Around six the following morning, the sun quietly started peeking it's rays of light through our bedroom window. Stephen was sitting in the lazy boy chair where he usually sat for prayer, wrapped up in his old, green, terry cloth bathrobe with his wool prayer blanket tucked in around his legs and up over his shoulders. After the long wrestling through the night, this is where he had ended up.

I had crawled back into bed, hugged up in a fetal position, trying to still pray, yet not really making any headway, most likely from sheer exhaustion.

The stillness of the early morning was filled with a quiet sense of "what will this day hold" hovering over us in an unspoken mist. Finally, the dreaded, anticipated hour of daybreak had come…and here we still were without an answer.

Both of us knew the other was awake, yet we both wanted to pretend the other was sleeping so no words would have to be spoken, no stupendous thoughts of deliverance would be expected or ingenious marathons attempted. Just silence as the aftermath from this strange, unforgettable night.

Quietly at first, then gaining volume as it came nearer was a sound somewhat familiar yet still unrecognizable to our overly strained ears. What was that?! The sound of frozen dirt crunching under tires as a car was slowly coming down our driveway. Who could that be this early in the morning, on this bizarre, trying day?!

Stephen hurriedly pushed the lazy boy into its upright position and slipped his worn bedroom slippers onto his chilled feet, all the while tightening the loose belt of his bathrobe snug around his waist.

I had taken the posture upon hearing the first sound of noise, of sitting bolt upright in bed, then hastily joining Stephen in putting on my old tattered, yet very comfortable robe. Whatever was going to happen, I didn't want to miss any part of it.

I could hear a medium loud rap on our door. Who could it be?! Stephen's feet were running hurriedly down the stairs to meet the persistent sound. Was it someone lost or in need? Why so early?

I could hear a woman's voice and then Stephen's startled reply...like he was going into some state of shock. My heart went up into my mouth in fear that it was bad news, something or someone else had fallen prey to trouble...yet, it didn't sound all bad as I began to detect the lightness in their voices.

I could hear Stephen thanking this woman with what sounded like a shaky, heartfelt tone, almost not really able to take it in tone. What was happening?!

Soon the door closed and I charged down the stairs needing to know what had happened. Stephen stood there with what looked like a check in his hands. His eyes were full of tears that soon began to stream down his ruddy cheeks.

A precious woman, who had come to a musical production once at our church and had given her heart to the Lord, was the lady at the door. She was Obie's wife. You remember, the man who had come to me with the beautiful bouquet of flowers?! Yes, his wife.

Sylvia, like her husband, wasn't coming to church regularly, yet her heart was tender towards the Lord. Several of her children and grandchildren had come out strong in their commitment to serve Him. Some had even gone on to Bible school, studying to be pastors.

She had explained to Stephen that she just couldn't get the thought out of her mind that Pastor needed $5000. The Lord hounded her, as she further explained, and specifically led her to bring the check on this morning, at this early hour, on her way to work. And now here Stephen stood with a check for $5000 in his hands. What a glorious miracle! God had heard every word and had seen every tear!

I walked across the room and fell into Stephen's trembling arms. There we were, both in our ratty bathrobes, like two old drunken sailors, weeping and rejoicing together almost as though we were in a dream...only it was true!

~

THERE WE WERE, BOTH IN OUR RATTY BATHROBES, LIKE TWO OLD DRUNKEN SAILORS, WEEPING AND REJOICING TOGETHER ALMOST AS THOUGH WE WERE IN A DREAM...ONLY IT WAS TRUE!

~

As our tears mingled in with our exclamations of joyful praise, Stephen came to his senses and told me to hurry and iron him a fresh shirt as he had to have the check in the right hands by nine o'clock.

Oh, the timing of the Lord! You have heard it said many times, God is never late and He is never early. He's always right on time! If you can stand the pressure and excitement of the ride, you will see His awesome Hand. He never will fail you.

What rejoicing there was when we came together as a church body that Sunday! Here was evidence of the fingerprint of God. We would go on with no idea of where our journey would lead us next.

~ PERSONAL REFLECTIONS ~

We could not spend money we did not have. We knew God was saying to us to stand. Make no mistake, Christians have battles and to give teaching that says they don't, is an out and out lie. When battles come, it is tempting to turn to the ways of the world to find answers. Getting a loan was a possible option, yet God in His all knowing closed every possible door to us for this. This was not to be our means of salvation in our time of crisis. (Nor should it be for us as individuals. Credit cards are not bad when used as a tool of convenience versus carrying wads of cash, but not to be used to run ourselves into hopeless debt). Romans 13:8 talks about those who spend money they do not have.

When the financial pressure is on, some Christians pray about it, but when they don't see an immediate provision, they quickly turn back to the ways of the world. We could not do this. God was teaching us that the delay of the provision was part of God's design for this particular season. We would not be allowed to short-circuit the purpose by finding some other quick cure for our problem.

~

GOD WAS TEACHING US THAT THE DELAY OF THE PROVISION WAS PART OF GOD'S DESIGN FOR THIS PARTICULAR SEASON. WE WOULD NOT BE ALLOWED TO SHORT-CIRCUIT THE PURPOSE BY FINDING SOME OTHER QUICK CURE FOR OUR PROBLEM.

~

The greater the delay, the deeper the work that God is performing in us. He wanted us to have our complete, absolute focus totally on Him. Isaiah 31:1 says, "Woe to those who go down to Egypt for help, and rely on horses, who trust in chariots because they are many, and in horsemen because they are very strong, but who do not look to the Holy One of Israel, nor seek the Lord!"

It was our choice: either we could continue to thrash in our own strength and attempts to meet this crisis or wait on God until He moved in the fullness of His glory and purposes.

God was specifically bringing us to a place of total, complete dependence on Him. We felt like we were going to die, yet He was in control all the time. I have often thought since this, how many other times in life have I felt like God has left me when He was right there all the time, waiting to be gracious to me in the circumstance I had found myself in?

This experience caused our faith to be enlarged to a greater ability to believe God in tough situations. The next hurdle seemed possible knowing God could do what we could not, in a very real way. Hard, pressing situations, yet great revelations and insight into the ways of God were coming. In order to receive the greater, one must be pressed into the harder. No tests, no victories!

THOUGHTS TO PONDER

♦ Is it wrong to try other doors, or should you completely sit still and look to God alone?

♦ Can you become out of balance by not trying doors and looking to God alone?

♦ What does it feel like to be totally shut up to God?

♦ What is the difference between coincidence and the supernatural timing and provision of God?

♦ What does a miracle do to your spirit? How does it feel to have heaviness suddenly be gone and your whole being shifting to a posture of great victory?!

THIRTEEN
~
FIRES AND FLOODS

We met the filing deadline and got the money into the hands of the right officials. Thus began the appearances we had to make in federal court and with a U.S. trustee. Then began a flurry of motions let loose by Deacon's lawyers. They were trying to say that we had filed for Chapter 11 in bad faith.

Meanwhile, our lawyers had us gathering and reviewing all the documentation we had so they could build our case. During this time period, Deacon brought more lawsuits against us. What a wild time in the old town tonight! We were hanging on tight trying to ride the old bull all the way home.

Then began the appointments in which depositions were taken. A deposition is where you appear before all the representing lawyers and a stenographer and are asked questions by both parties who are in dispute. You are under oath as when you give testimony in a courtroom, to tell the truth.

Stephen had to sit for hours and be questioned over all kinds of information. Deacon, his wife, and some of his workers were brought in to give deposition. Some of their stories became very cloudy under questioning. Their memories weren't quite as sharp as one would have expected.

Some of them were very uncomfortable with their former pastor sitting there listening. Stephen had led them to the Lord and had personally discipled them. Now they worked for Deacon and their faith was in where their bread was buttered. I'm sure it was a taxing time for them. Emotions, paychecks and human reasoning can pay a heavy toll when mixed together under the right conditions.

During this time, our lives became, what should I say…nervous. Some may ask why. Let me give you an example. One night during our dinner time, the phone rang. We usually tried to avoid answering it during our meal, but if the meal was almost over, I would leave the table and catch the incoming call.

I went to the phone and said hello. A man's voice was on the other end of the line. He gruffly asked me if we had a big, yellow bus out in back of our house. I answered with questioning in my voice, yes, we had a big yellow bus sitting out in back of our house.

Our youth group had worked hard to raise money for that bus - car washes, bike-a-thons, bottle drives. Endless efforts were made by these teens so they would have transportation to their events and special trips without having to ask parents to take time off to drive them there.

The next thing I heard coming from the phone was this curt, terse voice saying, "Well, you better go take a look at it." Then with a mocking, sarcastic laugh he continued on, "This is from Deacon!"

I quickly ran to the dining room where Stephen was finishing the last bites of his dinner. I was deeply upset, needless to say, I think at the time more heated than afraid. I blurted out what had been said during this distressing phone call.

The entire family rushed out to where the youth bus was parked. Sure enough, some brutal individual or maybe even two, had taken a heavy piece of metal or wood to our dear bus. The front windows were smashed in. The motor had taken some damaging blows as well. Toilet paper had been strewn all over it, inside and out. The back door hung open, flapping back and forth in the wind.

I stood there infuriated! How could they do this?! Who would believe us if we told them?! Could this kind of thing really be happening?! How could someone even come under the banner of Jesus and do this to other people?! But, here it was happening.

We telephoned the state troopers and they came, looked the damage over, and tried to find some evidence of who might have done it. There were no clues. I told them about the threatening phone call, and they recorded all the information in case something else was to occur. They were a little shocked and amazed themselves at the cruelty involved in this base deed.

We were concerned from that time on of even our phone lines being tapped. We were very careful what we said over them. We were always looking in our rearview mirrors to see if anyone was following us and we tried to always travel with at least one other person with us. If someone could do such violence once, wouldn't it stand to reason that they may attempt to do something again?

We entered into a reclusive world of paranoia. Never had we been around cruel, threatening people or circumstances. I'm sure this is what the devil had planned to happen; get us so afraid, that we would be paralyzed with fear, too afraid to retaliate or protect ourselves.

Thank God we had enough common sense not to let this happen. We began to dig deeper in God and in prayer and began listening more intently, moment by moment for His leading and direction. He was our survival life line. Isaiah 59:19b says, "When the enemy shall come in like a flood, the Spirit of the Lord will lift up a standard against him and put him to flight (for He will come like a rushing stream which the breath of the Lord drives)." Psalm 29:10 tells us, "The Lord sat as King over the deluge; the Lord (still) sits as King (and) forever!" There were heavenly lessons that had to be learned. God never promised us we would not know persecution. He did say though that He would be with us through it. He would reveal Himself to us as Lord over the floods of persecution.

The pressure of everything around us seemed to be trying to close in. We couldn't plan for tomorrow. It was enough to try to get through today. We never knew where the next turn in the road would take us.

$\sim$

GOD NEVER PROMISED US WE WOULD NOT KNOW PERSECUTION. HE DID SAY THOUGH THAT HE WOULD BE WITH US THROUGH IT.

$\sim$

Some days we had a faint ray of light and we would put our hands out to touch it hoping it would lead us onward and out of our troubles. But then the ray would dissipate and disappear right before us. The short distance which this ray of hope seemed to have moved us forward, felt like it had been retrieved from our grasp and we were again standing in gloom and darkness.

The thought at least a hundred times a day would come to your mind, "When will this end?" or "Will it ever end? Will I have a regular life again? Will I ever enjoy the normal things again like my family and the everyday happenings of their lives, or chatting over tea with nothing in particular to discuss with friends, just small talk?"

It wasn't just for a few days or months that we lived like this. It was years. The struggle to come to a settlement would not be quickly reached. There was a long, hard road to walk and when you thought you had gained a little momentum over a steep hill, you would then see before you at least two more tall mountains ahead to climb that had been hidden from your view from where you last stood.

Psalm 97:3a says that "Fire goes before Him." Psalm 50:3 says, "Our God comes and does not keep silence; a fire devours before Him and round about Him a mighty tempest rages." God was in the very middle of all of this. He knew where He was leading us. The Chief Shepherd always does. We didn't like this season of overwhelming floods and raging fires, but they were nothing to God. They never are.

~ PERSONAL REFLECTIONS ~

When the nation of Judah had Assyria rise up against them, they had a difficult time seeing God. All they could focus on was Assyria. It was during this time of upheaval that God caused Isaiah to pen the words, "For thus says the Lord God, the Holy One of Israel: 'In returning and rest you shall be saved; in quietness and confidence shall be your strength.' But you would not," Isaiah 30:15. These are tremendously challenging words in view of the fact that Assyria was breathing their hot breath down Judah's back. Let's analyze this verse for a moment. "In returning"—God is testing them to see if they will leave off pursuing other solutions. He is saying to them "Come back from Egypt, come home to Me, press into Me, be reminded of My plans for you, plans of good intentions and let your expectation be wholly from Me."

"And rest"—God was basically telling them to "Chill. Relax. Stop panicking. Give Me the time I want to work and learn to wait for Me to act." Judah said, "but Lord, did You notice the marching army headed this way?! We've got to do something!" And God said very simply, "Do nothing."

"In quietness"—the same word is used in the Word to describe wine that "settles" on its lees (Jeremiah 48:11). As wine is in process, it is placed on a shelf in total stillness so that the miniscule particles can settle to the bottom. So God is literally saying, "Settle down."

"And confidence"—This word thematically corresponds with the word "returning" like God is saying, "You need to regain the assurance and absoluteness that I will take care of you. Unbelief and fear can burglarize us of our confidence, and it's time to return and renew, refresh yourself in your stand of faith in who I AM, and in what I have spoken in promise to you in My Word."

THOUGHTS TO PONDER

♦ Why does God make us wait in total silence allowing the enemy to surround us on every side?

♦ Are those who would do us evil under the control of God or because of their free will can they move past His boundaries of protection?

♦ Should there have been a major confrontation with a greater pursuit of righting the wrong that had been done against the youth of the church? What response should leadership have given to them?

♦ What damage is done to young people when they see such things played out before their eyes? Do they necessarily need to become bitter and twisted or can God teach them deeper truths through these trying experiences?

♦ What do you think of the Scripture Isaiah 30:15 "In quietness and confidence shall be your strength?" Have you ever experienced circumstances where the Lord led you to live out this verse?

FOURTEEN

RED TAIL LIGHTS
IN THE DARK

Within time, a vote was to be put before the congregation as to whether they wanted to stay in their present denomination, explaining that the voting members had to all agree to leave if we were to continue with this vision and finish the facility as God had directed. We were on a deadline with the denomination and had to work within certain dates, or they would move in and try to take everything. So much for brotherly support and unity! Even in this devastating blow, God was working out a higher purpose which we could not see. He was taking us into a greater freedom than we had ever known. It was just very difficult to understand at the time.

The pressure of everything began to take a toll on Stephen. Professionals have since told us, that under such crises, you either cave in at the very beginning, as I had, or you crumble later on down the road, so to speak, being in a post trauma status mentality.

I remember Stephen calling me one day from work, and blurting out that he had to get away. Now! He couldn't take the pressure anymore. I asked where he wanted to go, and he replied, he didn't know, just that he had to get out of here. He came home, packed his truck with enough clothes for several weeks.

We both knew even though we weren't saying it out loud, that the date for the congregational vote was fast coming upon us. I knew he felt tremendous pressure from this as well as every other critical outbreak around him. He was like a fire fighter who had fought too many shifts

～

HE HAD TO GET OUT OR DIE.

～

in the middle of a raging forest. He was out of steam, no life left within him and no clean smoke free air to gulp down anywhere he turned. He had to get out or die. I knew he didn't want burden me with the responsibility to walk the church through this, but he was scared for his own survival. Leave and work out his feelings, thoughts, and concerns, sorting and rearranging these many cans of worms, or stay and crumble? I could sense his deep, inner wrestling.

We worked out the paperwork and specific instructions were written down for me to follow. Removing our congregation from this denomination had to be done right or legal problems, big legal problems could come on us down the road. I, too, was feeling the weightiness of the situation. We rehearsed the steps several times for me to be sure of its clarity.

He just couldn't stay around to go through this again. I knew he was very close to cracking. My heart was bleeding inside for him, yet I was helpless. I wasn't all that strong myself, yet there seemed to be a gentle grace that had descended down over my mind and spirit. God was there.

I watched the red taillights of his truck as they moved down the long driveway, holding our baby and thinking, "Where is he going? When will I hear from him again? What is going to happen to us next?" My soul seemed to be sucked into a deep, utter darkness as I watched those taillights become little tiny dots and then vanish as simultaneously the sound of his rough, choppy truck motor faded into a blurred, soundless oblivion, yet...over all of these uncontrollable emotions and nauseating fears, there was a gentle blanket of all encompassing, supernatural peace falling softly and soundlessly over me.

~ PERSONAL REFLECTIONS ~

Those times in life come to us all when what we thought would or could not ever happen somehow happens. Stephen had always been so strong for the children and me. He was our shoulder to cry on...the pillar of strength for the family. He was the one to finish out the gruesome task of walking through those last services. He was the one to have to sign when the liens were delivered. He was the one having to make the arrangements to hold services at the motel. He was the one looking out not only for his struggling family, but for all of the precious sheep from his flock. I'm sure he wrestled with himself many times whether he was leading them in the right direction.

~

I WATCHED THE RED TAILLIGHTS OF HIS TRUCK AS THEY MOVED DOWN THE LONG DRIVEWAY, HOLDING OUR BABY AND THINKING, "WHERE IS HE GOING? WHEN WILL I HEAR FROM HIM AGAIN? WHAT IS GOING TO HAPPEN TO US NEXT?"

~

Now here he was with something tremendously shaky going on deep in his inner being...a frightening feeling having to get away from it all. When pushed to the brink or stretched to the utmost elasticity of the mind, what does one do no matter how strong they have been in the past? You do what you have to do to survive. That ancient mechanism kicks in with us all. And so it was with Stephen. He had to get away from this camp of distress if only for awhile.

I, on the other hand, had felt a certain grace come over me from the Lord. After wrestling my own depression and unfulfilled expectations to the ground with the help and enabling of the Holy Spirit, I now had to stand by as Stephen conquered his own demons. He had stood faithful as head of his home—priest, provider, and protector. Sanity and stability were slipping away from him, barely at the precarious tips of his inner fingertips.

What was he to do? What was I going to do? Trust....abide in **His** quietness, **His** confidence...enter **His** rest.

THOUGHTS TO PONDER

♦ What does it feel like to come to the end of a struggle, still not having answers?

♦ Is it wrong to get away from it all for awhile?

♦ Is it weakness in leaders to recognize their own wounds and their own need for solace?

♦ Is the church equipped to minister to leaders in distress?

FIFTEEN

~

EVIL NO MORE

How do I explain the deep, black sense of doom the enemy sent out against our souls? I read in Ephesians 6:12, "For we do not wrestle against flesh and blood, but against principalities, against powers, against the rulers of the darkness of this age, against spiritual hosts of wickedness in the heavenly places." This is not a fun place to be at...uncomfortable in a weird, quirky way in your spirit without any sight of relief in the near future.

I was an avid reader, and had read many missionary stories about demonic warfare. In these books, they would describe the many days and long wearying nights of wrestling in prayer, just to survive. They would tell of the dear price that had to be paid in wrestling intercessory prayer to see spiritual breakthroughs over the various mission fields they had been called to.

Up to this point, in our sphere of experience, we had only warred against lower level demonic spirits in our ministry. We both were disciplined people of consistent prayer. Daily, we would set ourselves aside to have a designated time with the Lord. We both understood to be successful in our personal lives and ministry we needed to go forward on our knees.

God was about to shift us into a more intense learning process. Oh, don't you love that word...process?! We were soon to figure out that when the Word says you have to "'wrestle' against principalities, against powers, against the rulers of the darkness of this age, against spiritual hosts of wickedness in the heavenly places," it meant just that and much more. Just what did it all entail? We didn't fully know, but we were about to find out.

The power of the demonic realm seemed to press in heavily against us. Our thoughts were constantly, (and when I say constantly, I mean constantly), under attack. I would fall asleep with battering, hammering lies from the enemy trying to infiltrate my weary mind. I would find myself, just barely starting to wake and upon recognition realize I was yet again being bombarded with an over-whelming sense of suffocating darkness and bottomless, sinking doom all around me. I had never experienced any-thing this consistently, horrifically evil before.

We would try to enter into prayer, and get momen-tary relief, yet within hours, sometimes minutes, in would rush this heavy demonic oppression of the enemy. God was allowing this to happen to force us into learning how to "wrestle" against our foe.

One night, as we both lay in bed, almost too quietly, (you know what I mean, when you both are struggling and neither one has any specific word of greatly needed en-couragement for the other), I turned my back to Stephen and softly opened my Bible. I desperately needed a word from the Lord.

I turned to Zephaniah 3:14-20. It is a passage of Scrip-ture that describes the joy of God's faithfulness. I began to cry as I read it and said to the Lord, "Can this really be true for us? Or am I just reading these words like so many times in the past?" Somehow I knew deep in my spirit, He was giving me a glimpse of His heart for us in our troubled situation.

The one verse in this passage that seemed to leap off the page right into my spirit was verse 15. It reads in the King James Version, "The Lord hath taken away thy judgments, He hath cast out thine enemy: the king of Israel, even the Lord, is in the midst of thee: Thou shalt not see evil any more."

I laid there quietly in bed and wept silently before the Lord, asking Him to plant that word deeply into my spirit. I asked Him to remove the ever-present fear of more evil coming against us.

A few months after this verse was given to me on that night, I was asked to be worship leader at a retreat led by two dear friends. I didn't know if I would be capable to lead myself into worship, let alone others. Yet, I packed my bags, and along with a small group of women from our church, headed out for Massachusetts.

After all of us had gotten settled in our room, there was a short time to fellowship before dinner. We all sat around on our bunks talking and sharing everything and anything that popped into our minds.

I began to share the one line out of this passage in Zephaniah that I felt the Lord had given me, "You shall see evil no more." No one else was in our room, only the women from our group. We talked about it a little bit and agreed to extend our faith to believe that God was speaking to us.

We ate our dinner together and then all of us went into the evening service. I led worship with a heavy heart. I didn't want to hinder what the Lord might want to do, so I tried to keep a cheery smile on my face, although my heart felt like it had a two ton boulder sitting on it.

I got through the worship time and tried to listen to my good friend, Iris bring the Word. She always had a powerful anointing and would most assuredly speak a challenging and timely message.

I seemed to be just sitting there in a misty, swirling fog. I could hear others around me responding and I would try to bring myself into attentiveness to receive what was being said, but I wasn't very successful. In and out my mind traveled like a run away ping bong ball in a carnival game.

Iris, at the close of her message, invited people to come and find a place of prayer around the front. I went to the piano and began to play softly while others sought the Lord. I was lost in my own thoughts, yet I continued to minister songs of encouragement and inspiration to help keep a sweet presence of the Holy Spirit while others were seeking Him.

When just about everyone had gone back to their seats or had wandered off to get a little something at the snack bar, I left the piano and quietly prostrated myself behind it, to be somewhat out of sight. I needed some time to cry my own heart out before the Lord.

As I lay there, I asked Him, "Is it true that we really are not going to see evil any more? Lord, I hurt so badly. Is there no balm in Gilead? Is there no healing for my bruised and broken spirit?"

Suddenly, I felt a tapping on my shoulder. It was my other dear friend, Jeanne, asking me if a few of the women still there around the altar could pray for me. Now, I don't know about you, but I am one to take all the prayer I can get. My reasoning is that it never can hurt.

~

"THE LORD WOULD SAY TO YOU, YOU WILL SEE EVIL NO MORE!"

~

They placed a chair out in front of me indicating I should sit down and those that were there, gathered around me. They began to pray. All I could do was sit there with my eyes tightly closed. I didn't even have the strength to join in, not even a little bit. Usually I was the one praying and speaking words of encouragement to others. How did I end up here, the one in such desperate need?

Iris began to pray and then she prophesied. She told me that God was providing a ram in the thicket for our church, that He had great provision all ready for us that we knew nothing about.

~

THEN SHE STOPPED AND CAME DETERMINEDLY BACK, PUTTING HER HAND ON MY HEAD AND SAID, "OH, YES! THE LORD WANTS YOU TO KNOW, THERE IS A BALM IN GILEAD!"

~

Now, brace yourself, because every word I'm about to tell you is true. She laid her hand on my head and said, "The Lord would say to you, you will see evil no more!" Well…every woman who had been in our room before service and had heard me share that Scripture about passed out! Some of them literally began to weep loudly and openly. Others began to shout for joy! Could it really be?! What a powerful confirmation from the Lord!

But that's not all! Iris seemingly finished prophesying, turned and started walking away. Then she stopped and came determinedly back, putting her hand on my head and said, "Oh, yes! The Lord wants you to know, **there is a balm in Gilead!**"

Something just broke wide open inside of me like a dam giving way when she said that. I had only just a few minutes before this special prayer, asked God if there was any balm in Gilead, not even five minutes before. Here He was responding and making Himself so personal and real to me! How could I ever doubt that He was not involved in what was happening?!

I sat there and wept and wept before the Lord. What a faithful God!

Needless to say, we all went home different than when we came! Great faith was arising within us. God was in control, no matter what the enemy tried to tell us or how viciously he would try to hinder and wipe out what God had spoken to us. We would always remember!

We began to see that God would speak loudly and clearly to us to help us withstand the onslaughts of the enemy who had targeted us as "wrestling" partners. I remember many times when I would begin to sag in my spirit. I would think back to that day at that ordained retreat, and remember the intimacy of the Lord. I then would take heart, encourage myself in the Lord and brace myself for the next round the adversary would surely try to bring.

The journey of the dark night of our souls was definitely a learning experience…especially allowing us to catch a glimpse into the supernatural realms… both good and evil.

~ PERSONAL REFLECTIONS ~

"And being in agony, He prayed more earnestly" Luke 22:44. How did Jesus respond when the pain increased? He sought God more earnestly. Being pressed into affliction naturally produces desperation within us. The choices in this state are to lash out at everyone and everything or to collapse and live in a state of depression. God would have us though, channel that desperation toward a fervent pursuit of His face. Jesus did this in His times of desperation. If you are really hurting, this is a safe and Christ-like response. Run to Him. Seek Him fervently. If you allow your desperation to push you into Christ, you will come to know Him in a more intimate way, more profoundly and deeply than ever before.

Paul said in 2 Timothy 1:12 "For this reason I also suffer these things; nevertheless I am not ashamed, for I know who I have believed and am persuaded that He is able to keep what I have committed to Him until that Day." Because of Paul's sufferings, he is able to say, "I know whom I have believed." First he believed, and then he came to know.

Instead of harming us, (which always is what it feels like to our soul), those wounds, those afflictions will make us seasoned veteran soldiers who will know His voice if even only spoken in the softest whisper. Many times God uses affliction to bring us to greater spiritual maturity. When we allow God to work His perfect work, affliction actually backfires horrifically in the devil's face, for it thus becomes a powerful springboard for great growth and maturity in the heart of the sufferer, equipping him to become a most lethal weapon in the hand of God.

I believe God was putting a full nelson on us while we were still young, bringing us into great restriction contrary to our will, so that we could enter into a maturity that would hopefully exceed our years of past experience, and thus help us to have many years of fruitful ministry. Affliction definitely was bringing us to a place of greater dependence and brokenness. It felt like every breath was a gift from the Lord. Isaiah 53:10 talks about the suffering of Jesus like this, "Yet it pleased the Lord to bruise Him; He has put Him to grief." The word for "bruise" is "crush." It pleased the Lord to crush Him. This isn't a personal delight to the Lord to cause pain. Yet it is God's pleasure to see what this crushing would produce. God identifies with our pain. Isaiah 63:9 says "In all their affliction He was afflicted." The Father doesn't enjoy the process of afflicting us, but He is pleased with the product. Psalm 16:8 says, "I have set the Lord always before me; because He is at my right hand I shall not be moved." I might be crushed and broken, but I do not have to be moved. If I continuously set the Lord always before me, I'll come through the breaking and will still be standing.

Jesus, while in the Garden of Gethsemane, sweat as it were, great drops of blood. His disciples were there very near to Him, yet they could not bare what only He could bare. Jesus, Himself had to pray through. He kept saying, "Father, I know that You hear Me." Yet He felt so all alone. The disciples, those who were most close to Him were sleeping, not able to stay awake. His Father was silent. I'm sure He felt so all alone in this dark place and agony of soul. It is to this place that the Lord will lead us also; not so He can have pleasure in abandoning us, but as the time has passes, we can know Him better and more intimately. I was to come to learn and understand that God stores up some of His greatest victories for the yielded vessels that have known the greatest brokenness.

I believe I have come to understand that we don't really know what it's like for the Lord to be the complete strength of our lives until our own heart and flesh have failed. It actually is a hard place to get to, but oh, so wonderful when you've once arrived. You enter into the Hebrews 4 rest and in all situations the peace of God that passes all understanding.

THOUGHTS TO PONDER

♦ Is there a different sense in the two types of warfare that can take place in the spiritual realm—carnal warfare, whether it be with your own flesh or carnal man, and the warfare spoken of in Ephesians 6, "with principalities and powers, rulers of darkness, and spiritual hosts of wickedness?" How is the warfare different or similar?

♦ Does God actually remove His presence in these seasons of desperation or does He simply hide Himself from you? Compare the sense of aloneness with the revelation of His presence as was told in this chapter.

♦ When God speaks so clearly to someone, how does this solidify their faith, especially in future times of dryness and quietness?

♦ How important is it to give what God is stirring in your heart even when you do not understand what it could possibly mean?

SIXTEEN

~

MIDNIGHT PRAYER

We continued to learn how to fervently cry out to the
Lord in prayer. Remember how Scripture tells us that Elijah
was a man of **fervent prayer**? Now in our lives, the fervency factor had really been turned up from ten to one
hundred on the degree scale.

The sense of spiritual warfare was now a regular way
of life. We weren't just going through our everyday rou-
tines; we were in **fervent prayer** even as we worked and
went about our daily duties.

Many nights up out of bed I would come and head
for the den. We called this room the "duck room" because
the decor had been done in ducks, even down to the lamps.
My husband used this den as a part-time study and it was
in this room I would find myself.

Often I would not have the words to pray what I
sensed was happening around me. I didn't have any answers, but was driven to press into God's face to listen and
to hear what maybe He would say concerning everything
that was happening.

At first during these nights alone with God, I would
cryout my own troubled emotions and deep, unspoken fears,
rehearsing all that had happened to us. It was a soul-search-
ing period of emptying me of me. It seemed the Lord was

just letting me lean on Him, telling Him all about it. He's a splendid listener.

Then He began to talk to me, ever so gently, about my own attitudes and the attitudes of our congregation. I began to take a good, long look at myself and all the negative thoughts and mean-spirited words I had spoken out of incensed anger and deep cutting hurt. Slowly, my brittle heart began to turn towards the Lord in tearful repentance for how I had reacted under all of these difficult situations.

We often think when we hear about others' testing, that it would be easy for us to stand tall and straight in the Lord if it were us, that we would never fail...until it really does happen to us. We respond like Peter did in Luke 22:33. It says, "And Simon Peter said to Him, Lord, I am ready to go with You both to prison and to death." Jesus had told Peter in verse 32, "I have prayed especially for you, that your own faith may not fail; and when you yourself have turned again, strengthen and establish your brethren."

~

IT'S LIKE WATCHING SOMEONE HAVE A ROOT CANAL AND WONDERING WHAT'S THE BIG DEAL, UNTIL WE HAVE PLACED OUR BACKSIDE DOWN INTO THE CHAIR.

~

We look at others and wonder why they seemingly fall so easily. It's like watching someone have a root canal and wondering what's the big deal, until we have placed our backside down into the chair. Then starts the sweaty palms, the cranked, strained neck and the tears forming ever so slowly behind our tightly squeezed eyelids, as we hear the sound of the drill headed towards **our** mouth. All of a sudden we are not quite so brave and all knowing!

When all hell breaks loose in my world, I have found it is best never to rely upon my emotions or my own rationalizations. This kind of thinking can be very deceitful. Trust only in the Word of God. This is the Rock that will not be shaken. Everything else will move, but the Rock, Christ Jesus will stand firm through any storm. Psalm 18:2 says "The Lord is my Rock, my Fortress, and my Deliverer; my God, my keen and firm Strength in Whom I will trust and take refuge, my Shield, and the Horn of my salvation, my High tower."

Those long nights of intercession actually became my training ground in learning how to know the Lord and His ways. I began to long for the solitude and quiet of the night. I would look forward to that time alone with God all day long. I would lay prostrate in front of the crackling fire, wrapped in a warm blanket. My worn Bible would not be far from me. It seemed that these night meetings with the Lord became my lifeline to survival.

I began to hear His Voice more clearly. It wasn't that I always saw immediate answers to my prayers, but I would get a deep peace over each area of struggle and a strong assurance of His Presence and deliverance, no matter what the future would seem to hold.

As time went on, the Lord asked me to intercede for Deacon and his family. I couldn't believe my spiritual ears! But then as the Holy Spirit began to bring specific Scriptures to my attention, I understood what He was telling me.

One of the passages the Lord directed my attention to was found in Romans 12:20,21. It reads, "But if your enemy is hungry, feed him; if he is thirsty, give him drink; for by so doing you will heap burning coals upon his head. Do not let yourself be overcome by evil, but overcome (master) evil with good."

This word "master" caught my attention. Could this be possible? Could I learn to yield myself to the Lord and allow Him to break me and mold me so I too could see evil mastered by good?

Another passage was found in Proverbs 24:17,18. It reads, "Rejoice not when your enemy falls, and let not your heart be glad when he stumbles or is overthrown, lest the Lord see it and it be evil in His eyes and displease Him, and He turn away His wrath from him (to expend it upon you, the worse offender)."

Such Scriptures were pointing all the fingers back upon my own heart. I was not accountable for anyone else, but I was accountable for me. And it seemed the Lord was saying He would not let me move on in Him until I had dealt with these wrinkled issues of my own soul.

As I began to take a long look at my many failures, my heart felt like it had been smitten. It isn't pleasant to look at yourself in the full light of His convicting Holy Spirit.

After confessing every word, thought and action that came to light, I then could begin to pray for Deacon from a totally different perspective. At first it was like spitting out old, dry sawdust. My mouth and brain had become accustomed to speaking negatively and sarcastically about him and all that had happened.

~

THE LORD WAS TELLING ME, "STOP IT! STOP IT RIGHT NOW, I HAVE MUCH BETTER FOR YOU.

~

The Lord very plainly and emphatically was simply telling me, "Stop it! Stop it right now, Meredith. I have much better for you. I have a way for you where there seems to be no way. Re-train your mind and your mouth. I care about every thought and every word you speak. I want you to speak words of life, not death. And I want you to remember that it all begins in your mind and what you allow yourself to think and dwell on."

This looked like an incredible challenge for me. Believe me; the tide of people around me was fully and completely against this way of thinking. They were deeply wounded. When someone is wounded and in pain, they will do and say what they feel they have to to protect themselves. As weak humans, we deal with struggles in a fleshly way, usually not immediately in God's way. God had to readjust my thinking concerning these who were close to me. I knew they too had grievously suffered yet it was not my place to judge them, or correct them harshly but to unconditionally love them and try to encourage them to reach out and trust God to work as He chose.

I will confess that I failed Him many times. Abruptly something would come up and I would fall into the old pattern of running my mouth pessimistically and harmfully, rather than speaking words of faith and healing. My flesh is strong. I thank God for these lessons. Now I look at those who are angry and retaliatory and realize the position they are in. I understand that they are probably seriously hurt and deeply wounded. I try not to take it personally and I choose not to be offended.

I must confess there are times when the enemy hits me out of left field and I slip. It's at those times I am glad the Lord said in Psalm 37:24, "Though he fall, he shall not be utterly cast down; for the Lord upholds him with His Hand."

As time went on, I stayed faithful to intercede for my enemy and I truthfully and sincerely became concerned for Deacon and his family. The Lord led me to pray that He would bless them. I know that may sound very strange to you, but didn't God speak this concept to us in His Word? Matthew 5:44 says, "But I tell you, love your enemies and pray for those who persecute you." The Lord spoke to my heart that if I would pray that, He and He alone would know just how to deal with them.

Deacon wasn't to be **my** problem. He was God's. My part was to release him in prayer by praying that God would bless him and pray this daily until I really meant it.

God, like the good Father He is, doesn't need me to tell Him how to discipline and deal with His other children. It's comical when one of our five children come to us and tells us we are slipping in not dealing with their brother or sister as they think we should. They don't know the whole story of all that is happening with their sibling and even if we took time to explain it to them, why should we have to? We are the parents, they are not. We know their brother or sister on a totally different level than they do. It is the same with God.

I felt the intercession increase in my heart as I began to comprehend what the Lord was teaching me. Even as Elijah had a mantle he used in prayer, I felt a mantle of intercession come down over my life. This season was a tough boot camp 101 in learning to die to myself and come alive to Him.

~

THE QUIET OF THE NIGHT HOURS; THE SENSE OF HIS HOLY PRESENCE; THE STILLNESS OF MY OWN SPIRIT DURING THOSE EVENINGS ARE SOMETHING I STILL LONG FOR. GOD COULD BE FOUND THERE. HE REVEALED HIMSELF TO ME THERE.

~

Others thought I was losing it when in fact I was gaining. Even as David learned in the cave of Adullam how to survive under the testing of the Lord, so were we. Madame Guyon, an old mystic author, teaches that if you will embrace the cross of Christ, even in suffering and times of trial, when the cross is finally removed, you will miss the Presence of the Lord you have come to cherish because of how He revealed Himself to you in this kind of season.

Everything about our lives and ministry was in question at this time, but it was becoming one of the most sacred seasons of deeper learning and greater maturing we had ever experienced. It was our testing time even as the mighty and strongest trees are the ones that have weathered the most violent storms and are formed into priceless violins that make stunningly beautiful music for the whole world.

The quiet of the night hours; the sense of His holy Presence; the stillness of my own spirit during those evenings are something I still long for. God could be found there. He revealed Himself to me there. That "duck room" became a sacred inner sanctum of divine experience. I don't believe I would have known Him as I have come to know Him today if it had not been for those long night hours alone with Him.

Could it be that He woos us into His holy chambers to speak loving counsel and specific direction to us there, yet we will not slow down and come aside when He calls? Does it take a colossal trial in our lives to cause us to press firmly against the veil of the Holy of Holies?

~ PERSONAL REFLECTIONS ~

When we receive fast answers I believe we will find very shallow benefits. Maturing in God takes time. Age really doesn't have much to do with it, but our yieldedness to Him does. I never knew such intimacy with God was

~

WHEN WE RECEIVE FAST ANSWERS I BELIEVE WE WILL FIND VERY SHALLOW BENEFITS.

~

possible. I believe today that I probably would not have set myself aside like I did during this season unless I had been painted in a corner so to speak. Why couldn't my heart have run after Him without such pressure having to be applied?

Today I am thankful for these lessons. In fact, I would agree with Madame Guyon *(Experiencing the Depths of Jesus Christ)* that I truly miss that place of intimacy and the depth of communion I felt through this time of trial.

THOUGHTS TO PONDER

♦ What do you think this saying means -"Choose not to be offended?" Is this easy or hard?

♦ Why is it necessary to be empty of yourself before God can speak in fullness to you the way His heart desires?

♦ What part does pride play in a person's heart? Is God trying to bring us to a place of powerlessness and nothingness? Why or why not?

SEVENTEEN
~
GOD HAS HEARD EVERY WORD

Day by day we learned to walk by faith. At times things would seem to develop quickly and at other times, things would seemingly move at a snail's pace. We never knew if we were going to continue to survive as a church.

One day in particular, Stephen came home with yet one more bad report of another needed amount of money for lawyers that we just didn't have. I tried not to look and sound discouraged in front of him. I tried to speak a few faith filled words of encouragement and to act like I had a solid confidence that God had everything under His control.

As soon as Stephen left the room, I stumbled up to our bedroom with tears streaming down my face, locked the door and threw myself across the bed. I cried out to God, "Haven't you even heard one word that I have prayed to You? Where are You and what are You going to do?"

No sooner had I raggedly cried these burning words from my lips when the phone began to noisily ring. I let it ring a few times in hopes that someone else in a better frame of mind than I would pick it up. I really didn't feel like talking to anyone.

No one (of course) would accommodate me. On the fifth ring I grudgingly answered. "Hello." "Hi, Meredith, this is Cindy." Cindy is a dear friend I grew up with back home in Maine. I hadn't heard from her in some time. She knew nothing about what was going on in our lives. I couldn't imagine why she was calling. She continued on.

"I was just finishing up my dinner dishes when the Lord so clearly spoke to me to call you with this word. I argued with Him to let me at least finish wiping down the table. He told me to call you right now and I'm standing here with my dish rag in my hand and water dripping onto the floor. This is what God wanted me to tell you: 'He has heard every word you have prayed since you first began to pray!'"

~

HE HAS HEARD EVERY WORD YOU HAVE PRAYED SINCE YOU FIRST BEGAN TO PRAY!

~

I couldn't believe my ears! God had spoken to me in a matter of a few moments just like a present dialogue taking place! Every bit of discouragement and weariness rolled off me like someone had quickly driven a one ton truck off my body at the speaking of that word!

Oh, how good God is! He knew I needed to hear something from Him or I was going to crumble. I just couldn't hold up any longer in my own finite strength.

I thanked Cindy profusely for her obedience, telling her she would never know this side of heaven what a blessing she had been to me at the exact moment I needed it.

Daniel explains God's faithfulness to him in just the same way in Daniel 10. Daniel had fasted for 21 days and had waited upon the Lord for his nation, listening for the answer to come.

An angel came to him when he was about all spent, in fact, the angel had to help him sit down on a chair and then help hold Daniel up to receive what he had to tell him. He told him to hang on. There was warfare going on in the heavenlies. God wanted Daniel to know He had heard every word Daniel had prayed since he had set his heart to seek God.

My heart, like Daniel's, was supernaturally touched. I could go on in His Strength.

~ PERSONAL REFLECTIONS ~

Zephaniah 3:17 says, "He will quiet you with His love." The "quiet" of Zephaniah 3:17 comes from the same root word in Hebrew as the "quietness" of Isaiah 30:15. It means to rest, be quiet, be still. The key to this is found in God's unfailing love. "He will settle you down with His love." He's the giver of this love; we are the receivers.

There are several ways God gives forth this love to us. First, He reveals His all-encompassing love to us. It is a very sovereign and hallowed act when He comes to us personally and speaks His love to us. It's totally captivating and altogether overpowering. All hell has broken out around us in our lives, but suddenly it doesn't seem to matter anymore. Refreshingly we realize, "He loves me, and is speaking directly to me!"

This is what quiets the heart. It is God making His reality known to us through His passionate affection for us. Romans 8:37 says, "Yet in all these things we are more than conquerors through Him who loved us." In what things are we more than conquerors? The text tells us, "tribulation, or distress, or persecution, or famine, or nakedness, or peril, or sword" (Romans 8:35). We more than conquer **in** all of these things. How? Through Jesus who loved us and gave Himself for us. Receiving this supernatural revelation of His divine love enabled me to overcome. He quieted me in the midst of the storm. The Scripture calls us "more than conquerors" because we taste of His great victory even before the battle is over.

We must remember that God wants to prosper us, and is good, kind and merciful all the time—even when we do not understand nor can we see the light at the end of the tunnel. He doesn't withhold His mercy to test us and see if we will trust Him. No, He is carefully merciful and good, even when wounding us. "Faithful are the wounds of a friend."

~

WE MUST REMEMBER THAT GOD
WANTS TO PROSPER US, AND IS GOOD,
KIND AND MERCIFUL ALL THE TIME.

~

The second way in which God quiets us with His love is by enflaming our hearts with our love for Him. He uses our crisis to perfect and mature our love for Him. He is using what you are going through right now to perfect your love for Him. Upon receiving this word from the Lord of how He had heard every word I had prayed since I began, made me feel like I did when I was a little girl settling down in the strong arms of my grandfather as he over and over again told me how much he loved me and wanted me to be near him. The old saying is true, "Father does know what is best."

THOUGHTS TO PONDER

♦ What does the phrase "more than conquerors" mean to you?

♦ Does God ever lose control of our situations or choose to ignore us?

♦ How important is it to be obedient to the Voice of God at the time He speaks to us?

♦ Does God always answer before midnight?

EIGHTEEN

~

THIS CHURCH HAS A RIGHT TO EXIST

Long days and nights of intercession were our routine and lifeline now. God was doing a deep work down to the very core of our beings, a work which was not easily understood by us.

After filing Chapter 11 to reorganize, the lawyers' work continued. It was a long drawn out process costing thousands of dollars.

It was hard for Stephen and Carl, who usually went with him, to sit in the same room with some of the same men they had worshiped with and hear them speak about what had happened in a totally different light. But testimony had to be given for the judge to be able to rule properly.

Finally the depositions were finished. Now was the time for all the findings to be brought before the judge. We had worked feverishly on our reorganization plan with our lawyers, drawing out to the very penny where we were going to raise the support needed to finish the building and begin holding services plus move the school into the building.

Our lawyers' bills were skyrocketing. Something had to culminate fast. We all, as a congregation were in constant prayer, meeting in homes weekly, believing God for His perfect will in this matter. By this time, we were all pretty much willing to go worship in a tent if that would be what He commanded. We had all come to the conclusion that a building is just that, a building. Our love for the Lord and one another became the overriding precedence of the day. We all just needed a sense of finality and closure to this never ending nightmare.

The day finally came when everything was to be presented to the judge. I, myself could not stand to go and sit through the agony and suspense of what the final outcome would be. Many of the congregation, bold souls that they were, faithfully went sitting together as one brave band of warriors in that courtroom that day. Stephen was glad for their steadfast support. He had to testify again before the judge, explaining everything, with the help of the lawyers to present our reorganization plan to him.

Deacon's lawyers charged we had filed in bad faith and our plan was not doable. You could feel the tension in the air like electricity. The intensity was so thick, you could cut it with a knife. Truly the prince of the power of the air was hoping for a huge victory in defeating us from carrying on and finishing our building, holding services and preaching the gospel of Jesus Christ.

I'm sure hell had paid big for front row seats to see the ending of this long, tedious battle. The enemy had placed high bets on our demise over the years and even up to this very moment. Yet God was God in it all.

Finally, the judge had heard all he needed to hear. Deacon's lawyers had argued and rebutted everything that could be turned and twisted over several times. Enough was enough.

The judge began, "I have heard all of the findings and have carefully gone over each piece of evidence. My conclusion is that **this church has a right to exist!** I will accept their reorganization plan as written." You could hear the church people collectively breathe out together a huge sigh of relief, gingerly holding back their boisterous shouts of praise and rejoicing for the victory God had given. Just outside the doors of the courtroom, the hallway immediately became a sacred tabernacle to celebrate the goodness of the Lord in the land of the living. Heartfelt bear hugs and sincere hallelujahs echoed and rang through the corridors of the courthouse that day.

Later stipulations were made as to when debts were to be paid off and when our plan was to be put in place. Deacon was not a happy camper. His every attempt to destroy us had been thwarted by the Lord. We were going to go on as a church working in the harvest field God had originally called us to. We knew it wasn't going to be easy, but hey, God had brought us this far and He would finish it.

Finally we had come to a definite crossroads. **We would survive!**

~ PERSONAL REFLECTIONS ~

Isaiah 30:26 says, "In the day that the Lord binds up the bruise of His people and heals the stroke of their wound..."

"I kill and I make alive; I wound and I heal." Deuteronomy 32:39

"Come, and let us return to the Lord; for He has torn, but He will heal us; He has stricken but He will bind us up. After two days He will revive us; on the third day he will raise us up, that we may live in His sight." Hosea 6:1-2

"Though I have afflicted you, I will afflict you no more; for now I will break off his yoke from you, and burst your bonds apart." Nahum 1:12-13

"For You, O God, have tested us; You have refined us as silver is refined. You brought us into the net; You laid affliction on our backs. You have caused men to ride over our heads; we went through fire and through water; but You brought us out to rich fulfillment." Psalm 66:10-12

These Scriptures bear witness to the deep waters we had to walk through. The Lord affirms in these verses that we will know deep waters; we will experience the fire. These terms are terms to describe trauma, depression, overwhelming difficulty, crisis, anxiety, and pressure. But instead of being totally destroyed by these things, God gives us His assurance that we will come out better for it.

Psalm 34:17 says, "The righteous cry out, and the Lord hears, and delivers them out of all their troubles." You must keep a steady guard over the purity and integrity of your life before God. You must continuously stand before God in consistent faithfulness and uprightness. You must diligently watch the issues of your own heart and allow the Holy Spirit to work His maturing work in you. It is to just such that this promise is given.

THOUGHTS TO PONDER

♦ What value should be placed on prayer in times like these?

♦ How important were the prayers of agreement throughout this trial?

♦ How do you guard your heart during trying times such as the depositions that Stephen and Carl had to attend?

♦ Does every Christian face such depths of trial as these verses describe? Is it always the hand of the Lord?

NINETEEN

THE LION'S HEART

After a year of liens and lawsuits, one on top of the other, we had come to the place where our reorganization plan under Chapter 11 was to be worked out. If this plan was accepted by the judge who had declared we had a right to exist, we would then come out of Chapter 11 and our two hundred thousand dollar bullet loan would be included under our reorganization plan.

If we had not filed Chapter 11, we would have been forced to liquidate all of our assets to pay off debt.

Deacon was not a happy camper over this turn of events. He had in his mind that he would be able to make good on his threats of buying us at one end of the street and selling us at the other. God had other plans.

Under this reorganization plan, we had to come up with a way to make money to show that we could reorganize and pay off these supposed liens and bogus lawsuits. We began to work on our tithing and giving records as well as to lay out the plans for a daycare to be established in the new facility.

We continued fighting the authenticity of these claims of owing Deacon close to one million dollars through the work of our lawyers. There were hours of depositions and meetings to help our lawyers establish paper trails and evidence contrary to Deacon's claims.

Stephen and I would stay up many long, tedious nights studying and typing needed information for the lawyers so they would be able to have things in order to make firm our case of unjust debt. All the while, we were still trying to finish the front of the church so that we could move out of the motel rooms where we were presently holding Sunday afternoon services. Most of the money that was coming in had to go towards keeping the lawyers moving forward.

Stephen had come off salary along with everyone else who had worked full time for the church. We still felt to hold to our commitment to pay a double tithe until the building was completed. We had no idea when we had knelt that day at the altar that Sunday morning that it would ever have taken so long to come to the completion of this project.

Now Stephen was off salary, working cutting wood, hauling stone and working construction. We did not have the assurance from week to week if the money would be there to pay our bills. Good news! God never failed us once. David, the Psalmist said, "I have been young and now I am old and I have never seen the righteous forsaken nor their seed out begging bread."

The cupboards would be almost bare and someone would "just happen" to have extra canned goods or vegetables to share with us. God never left us hungry or without.

Even our Christmases were blessed. We never felt the lack or missed a beat. Our tree was loaded every year with the blessings of the Lord. Our church family was still able to give out to those less fortunate even though they too were making great sacrifices to keep the work of the Lord going.

Finally, the big day came when Stephen and I were called in to meet with all the lawyers involved on both sides. The depositions were over and a large part of the needed research had been done to go to court. Deacon was anxious to make a settlement. He didn't seem to want all this to be dragged out for the public to see under the watchful eye of the court system.

We, on the other hand, did not have the finances to continue to feed the lawyers funds to do this. We already were in debt to them for quite a large sum. So, here we were being called in to try to negotiate a settlement agreement.

Stephen is a tremendously strong individual, but put under immediate direct pressure to make decisions quickly, this doesn't come easy for him.

As we entered the room, we were asked to take seats at a huge mahogany conference table. As I sunk down into the blush leather seat I was directed to, I sent up an urgent prayer to the Lord. "Lord, please be with us. Give us your direction." I remember my hands feeling slippery with sweat and my heart beating like it was going to race out of my chest.

Deacon's lawyers, (we were to come to understand), had been put on a conference call with their voices coming out of monitor boxes sitting on the table. They were none the less imposing.

All of our lawyers were present, both our bankruptcy lawyer and our corporate lawyer and their underlings. I rapidly calculated in my head how much per hour we were paying out for their expert counsel. It wasn't pretty.

Soon the long awaited negotiations began. The first lawsuit presented was discussed extensively. Stephen seemed overtly fidgety, shifting uncomfortably back and forth in his own plush chair. Deacon's lawyers would come off forcefully bellowing through the imposing monitors demanding harshly that we pay this lawsuit in full. The little boxes seemed to ring and vibrate with their severely forthcoming demands.

The lawyers would look questioningly at Stephen who seemed to have drifted off into another world. He wouldn't speak out any responses. He would barely make any eye contact with them.

After numerous attempts to exact answers from him, they then began to look at me. I thought to myself, "Oh no! What is going on? Why isn't Stephen giving them answers to the questions they're posing?!" Then it all came to me. He wasn't able to handle this immediate pressure. He always seemed to need time to mull things over, never making snap decisions.

Stephen backed his now uncomfortable plush chair away from the conference table, stood up and began to pace back and forth behind our chairs. When my husband gets frustrated, he has this way of messing his hair up so that it is standing straight up in the air. It gives him this intense "Einstein look." He gets rather scary looking! Next as he doggedly began to pace like a caged animal, he managed to twist a button off his shirt. Ping! Like a misfired bullet it popped off and rolled onto the rugged floor. My heart went out in sympathy to him. I knew how hard he had labored to get all of this paperwork together, months and months of researching and writing and rewriting. He had had to sit in all of those lengthy depositions and attend meeting after meeting with the lawyers collectively and separately. Now here we were and he couldn't make another decision, especially ones of these vast proportions.

I felt a hot, holy anger and a powerful overwhelming boldness well up in my overly stretched spirit. The lawyers began to look to me. You could almost silently read under their cool veneer a panic stricken look wanting to surface as they saw their main man losing it.

I began to ask Deacon's lawyers in a loud, controlled firm voice (coming from who knows where) to explain why they felt different suits should be paid in full. Then miraculously all of those nights of typing and discussing the evidence with Stephen paid off. My thoughts were beginning to come very clearly. I actually knew exactly what I was talking about!

~

I REMEMBER PLACING MY HANDS FIRMLY ON THAT MAHOGANY CONFERENCE TABLE AND DETERMINEDLY RETORTING, "THAT LAWSUIT ISN'T EVEN ON THE TABLE. THROW IT OUT!"

~

Our flustered lawyers began to immediately perk up. Deacon's lawyer would call out an amount such as $250,000 in this one particular lawsuit for example. The boldness of God came down over me like a bath of hot oil. I remember placing my hands firmly on that mahogany conference table and determinedly retorting, "That lawsuit isn't even on the table. Throw it out!" And guess what! Out it would go!

This happened several times during these intense negotiations. And then as the bantering went back and forth, other suits were settled at half their initial value. We made it crystal clear when all was said and done, that it was to be written in each document that we were returning Deacon's donations. These real or make believe amounts were never, ever intended to be debt. We had never intentionally gone into debt the way he was claiming. We knew his companies had given large gifts of money, but at this time in the story, who knew what the whole truth really was other than God Himself.

When all was said and done, we walked out of there with a settlement of paying back Deacon's **donations** for about half of his original claims of liens and suits that he declared we owed him. It was doable!

I thank God for His awesome Presence that came in such a powerful way that day in that room. I will never forget His Lion's Heart that He imparted to me at that exact moment that mine had turned into a puddle on the floor. His Word is true. He never leaves us or forsakes us! Jesus arises within us to accomplish His plan. I know beyond a shadow of a doubt that I can always trust Him no matter how difficult the circumstances may become.

~

GOD TELLS US IN HIS WORD BEFORE THE TRIAL EVEN COMES, THAT HE HAS ALREADY MADE A WAY OF ESCAPE FOR US.

~

God tells us in His Word before the trial even comes, that He has already made a way of escape for us. The exit signs have to be installed in a building before anyone can occupy it. God always makes a way of escape before we ever find ourselves in the midst of the problem. We have to learn to let Him lead us through the testing and not give up and quit halfway through it.

Now we had to get court approval for this long awaited settlement. There seemed to always be another tedious mile to walk, but at least we were moving forward led like the Israelites out of Egypt, the pillar of cloud by day and the pillar of fire by night.

~ PERSONAL REFLECTIONS ~

Those long nights of typing and hashing and rehashing documents, financial statements and church records of every kind, eventually paid off. But at the time when the needed discipline of organizing and putting things in order was the mode for the day, it felt like we were in an impossible never ending nightmare. Yet we faithfully plodded through to cross ever "t" and dot every "i". God knew what He was working all along. We both needed to have the information under our belts.

Job 23:10 says, "But He knows the way that I take (He has concern for it, appreciates, and pays attention to it). When He has tried me, I shall come forth as refined gold (pure and luminous)." Easy to quote, hard to remember and put in practice during those wearisome seasons of trial.

I see so many Christians who know they have experienced salvation, put have absolutely no joy or peace on the road of daily life. If I were unsaved, I would not want what they have. A hangnail becomes a major crisis. They do not enjoy their daily walk with God because they have not caught a glimpse that God is in every moment of our lives, orchestrating and arranging and rearranging it to bring forth the greatest fruitfulness and fullness of His purpose. He knows what He is doing…all the time, even in dull, boring routine. Even though you may not understand why or for how long you may have to walk a certain road, know that as you stay yielded to Him, He will faithfully guide.

~

EVEN THOUGH YOU MAY NOT UNDERSTAND WHY OR FOR HOW LONG YOU MAY HAVE TO WALK A CERTAIN ROAD, KNOW THAT AS YOU STAY YIELDED TO HIM, HE WILL FAITHFULLY GUIDE.

~

Because it gets dark during a storm does not mean that the sun has gone forever. It **will** shine again. Stay constant in the plodding He has placed you in knowing deep down in your spirit that He is in total control, working all things out for good, even the plodding.

In times of crisis, the Holy Spirit can arise and speak powerfully through us. He doesn't just operate through teaching and preaching but under times of great duress. He said, "Lo, I am with you always." I'm especially seeing

His faithfulness in situations I dislike and really want no part of. Thank God for His constancy and omnipotence towards us.

THOUGHTS TO PONDER

♦ Discuss the importance of keeping good paper trails.

♦ Why does God require seasons of plodding in the dark?

♦ Do you think miracles are happening more often than we recognize around us, yet we are stuck in thinking of them only happening in ways that have been rehearsed to us?

TWENTY

~

HAVE THINE OWN WAY, LORD?

Various times during our testing periods, it seemed that God allowed us to be tried from many different directions at the same time.

During this strenuous season of difficulties, one of the mainstay books I kept near me was *Experiencing the Depths of Jesus Christ* by Madame Jeanne Guyon. One of the principles she teaches is that we must see God in everything. Sometimes God comes to us in a beautifully wrapped package and then at other times, He comes to us in an old, brown paper bag. Both gifts are equally from Him.

Another concept that seemed to speak loudly from her writings was the practice to receive each moment as it is lived as having come through Him. I began practicing this discipline and my faith began to grow steadily. A new profound peace settled its roots deep in my sore spirit. I was able to receive the diverse tests without panicking and becoming overly distraught. I was beginning to see Him in everything that came our way, beautifully wrapped or not. I thank God for the saints of old and their anointed writings.

My spirit seemed to be going forward, but my body began to do some strange things under the constant stress. It didn't matter where I was, if someone started talking to me concerning the church, I would feel my nose and throat begin to itch and tighten. Then within minutes, I would start sneezing. The more they talked, the more I sneezed. It would almost seem comical if it hadn't been so seriously taxing.

~

***MY SPIRIT SEEMED TO BE GOING FORWARD,
BUT MY BODY BEGAN TO DO SOME STRANGE
THINGS UNDER THE CONSTANT STRESS.***

~

I would say to myself, "What are you doing? You can stop this, so just stop!" It was to no avail. I would be in the middle of a service with the whole congregation there, and someone begin to speak or pray about the church and its challenges, and I would begin to sneeze. It really was laughable! Everyone would begin to stare at me. I knew they were thinking, "What's wrong with her? Why doesn't she just stop? Or why doesn't she just go out?"

I felt horribly embarrassed, especially the times someone would have to drive me home, sneezing all the way, so I could lie down and put cool clothes over my face and take a pill to help the sneezing subside. I would literally have to fall asleep for these sudden attacks to stop.

I remember one evening when Stephen wanted to talk to all five of our children to explain something that was happening with the church and its battles. We tried to keep a spirit of peace and tranquility at home and give the kids only the bare basics so they would not have to live in any sense of anxiety. We knew we couldn't totally shelter them, but we wanted to do the best that we could that was in our control.

I remember him calling everyone into our bedroom. As usual, they all piled on the bed around me. It was a little crowded, but we were all used to that.

As Stephen began to gently explain the challenges we all were facing, I began to sneeze…one sneeze, then another, then another. "Stop it, Meredith!" I would say to myself. I would hold my breath and then out would come yet another forceful sneeze blowing even louder under the built up pressure. I knew my family was trying not to get upset or stare. I could sense their silent concern and feel the gaze of their wondering eyes.

I just buried my head in my pillow and silently sneezed and softly cried so my family would not know my pent up frustration. It was enough for them to understand and carry what was being said, without them having to worry over their sneezing, wheezing mother.

Finally the sneezing attacks became unbearable and totally uncontrollable. Upon a visit to my doctor, he recommended a specialist who announced to us some big, long medical name for my condition. The bottom line, he told us was that the sneezing was triggered by stress. Wow! What a revelation! He assured us that as soon as the stress would leave, then the condition would probably leave with it. Yeah!

The specialist put me on a topical steroid to daily spray up my nose and some pills to take only when needed. Thank God the medicine did help. I was able to function again but I did not like having to be on this medication.

God eventually would heal me completely of this problem. As of today, I am medicine free and sneeze free except for the occasional pepper or cold sneezes.

Something this trial has taught me is that our bodies can act uncontrollably different than normal when they are put under great stress. Each one of us is wired differently. I no longer am quick to judge others who are struggling with physical challenges beyond their control.

The tendency before this physical challenge was to have a flippant attitude of "Oh, why can't they discipline themselves to change?" Or, "They must be lazy and undisciplined. How can God use them?" Or, "They must not be a very strong individual to become susceptible to that problem."

Now my heart goes out to that one and I begin to pray for God's pathway of healing to come for them. God causes me to remember the heartache and the heavy embarrassment of the physical burden He allowed me to bare for a season. I no longer am anxious to make comment and offer my astute criticisms of others who I have no understanding of, nor will I ever walk in their shoes for even one day.

I am reminded of the story I once heard of a Sunday School superintendent who was very upset with one of her teachers who left his class at the very stroke of the end of the Sunday School hour. It wasn't that he didn't do a good job with his class, but that it just bugged her that he left so abruptly every Sunday. Why couldn't he stay and be an example for his students by being in the morning service?

Finally, in all her huffiness, she called the Sunday School teacher aside and informed him that he must resign his teaching position. She had come to the conclusion that he wasn't setting a good enough example for his students because he wasn't staying for morning worship. He sadly handed over his teaching books and supplies. Then he made his exit with his head hanging down.

The next day, the Sunday School superintendent braggingly boasted of her toughness in dismissing this certain teacher from his position. The conversation went strikingly silent. The person to whom she was speaking, then began to explain that this man's wife was an invalid and for him to even leave her those few hours to come and teach his class, was a big sacrifice for both of them. There was no way possible for him to be able to stay and attend service after class without endangering his wife.

The Sunday School superintendent was humiliated and embarrassed by her own brashness. She went to the man and his wife and humbly apologized asking him to take back his class.

This is the kind of lesson the Lord deeply taught me by allowing me to suffer physically while walking through one of the most difficult times in our ministry. I know now these were lessons I needed to deepen my understanding of the heart of God. He sees us all the time and understands what we are thinking and feeling. He will not allow more than we can bear. Oh, it may feel like you can't bear anymore, but trust His guiding Hand. He knows, sees and understands every part. Proverbs 37:23 in the Amplified says, "The steps of a good man are directed and established by the Lord when He delights in his way and He busies Himself with his every step." Be assured God cares the same for you right now, right where you are and what you are going through.

~ PERSONAL REFLECTIONS ~

If I am to be a true servant of the Lord and not self-destruct, then God must initiate by doing a tremendous breaking and then emptying in my heart. One cannot say to God, you may work in this area of my life, and not this one.

I have wrestled with the concept that I have matured greatly over the years. It simply isn't as true as I would like it to be. The only wisdom I receive is moment by moment and day by day, for you see, who alone but God knows what the future holds over our physical health and spiritual walk?

I know most of us will not want to hear this, but there are times God uses affliction to thrust us into another dimension in Him. Samson was thrust into just such a dimension when his eyes were put out. It wasn't until he lost his eyes that Samson actually began to see. This tragedy catapulted him into the realm of the Spirit. We will stand at the altar and sing "Have Thine Own Way, Lord," or "I Surrender All," and truly think we mean it until life begins to happen and God allows trial and testing to come our way. We must learn that God truly is in control of everything, the good and the bad. He is teaching and enlarging us, preparing us for the new wine He has for us.

Paul wrote in Colossians 1:24, "I now rejoice in my sufferings for you, and fill up in my flesh what is lacking in the afflictions of Christ, for the sake of His body, which is the church." Rather than us keep silent concerning our afflictions, could it be that God wants us to use these experiences to encourage someone else in present similar challenges that God is with them and will bring them through also?

THOUGHTS TO PONDER

♦ What does affliction do to one's spirit?

♦ Can affliction be an attack of the enemy? If so, why does God allow it?

♦ In Samson's case, do you think God used his affliction to turn him around? Could there have been an easier way?

TWENTY-ONE
~

THE TRYING OF OUR FAITH AGAIN

Another miraculous happening during this dark night of our souls, began early one sunny morning. For some reason, (obviously known later as the leading of the Holy Spirit), I felt strongly impressed that Stephen and I were to pray over our children, laying hands on each one asking God for special protection throughout the day.

~
I KNEW IT WAS VERY IMPORTANT TO
"MIND THE CHECKS" OF THE HOLY SPIRIT.
~

It was our normal habit to pray protection over them every day anyway, but this day, I felt we were to do it differently. I knew it was very important to "mind the checks" of the Holy Spirit.

We called them all into the living room and one by one we prayed asking God for His blood covering and angel guard protection to be over them to keep them from all danger and evil people. I felt a release that we had done what God had wanted us to do and we all went about our busy day.

That evening, we were hosting a prayer meeting for the church family at our home. I had wanted to get our younger children bathed and as near ready for bed before everyone came to pray as possible.

Jordan, the baby of the family, had had her bath and hair washed. For some unknown reason, I had wanted to put sponge rollers in her hair to curl it. Her hair was a pretty honey blonde and she looked so beautiful with it curled. She had sat patiently playing with a doll while I rolled it for her and then she had scurried off to go outdoors and play with some of the church children who had already arrived with their parents.

On the back of our house was a cellar door that had been propped up with a stick. Jordan and some of her playmates had decided it would be great fun to see how far they could spit down into the cellar. As the children were enjoying their little game, Jordan leaned up against the stick holding up the heavy cellar door. Somehow it was jarred from its position of bracing the cellar door. **Wham!!** Down on Jordan's little head, full force slammed this seventy pound cellar door!

One of the older teenagers playing out on the lawn, saw what had happened and quickly scooped her up and ran with her into the house. I'm not one to usually lose my cool, but this was something I had never seen before and this was **my** baby!

The skin on her forehead had fallen to either side of her head. Blood was covering her entire face. We were looking at the white bone of her forehead. There is no muscle over this part of the face to hold the skin in place. I lost it! I simply did not know what to do. I screamed for Stephen to come. Francis, one of the church women, was a nurse and had arrived early for the prayer time together. She quickly took charge by pulling the skin up where it had slid down and steadily began to hold it in place adding pressure with her hand to help stop the bleeding at the same time. Warm cloths were used to wash as much of the blood off Jordie's face as possible. Poor little thing! She looked so pitiful!

Stewart, another man coming to the prayer meeting, was just pulling up the drive. Stephen, now holding Jordan (with Francis marching steadily beside him and myself going before them to make a walkway for them to come), hurriedly jumped into Stewart's van, all the while explaining to him the emergency. Stewart swiftly backed his vehicle out and we sped as quickly as possible to the Medical Center.

We prayed over that little girl all the way to the hospital. We were told later that the folks back at the house immediately joined hands and began to intercede, especially our oldest son, Benjamin. People there said that Ben, a young teen at the time, fervently prayed for his baby sister beseeching God to spare her little life.

My mind was a blur, as if we all had just entered into a blistering fog that had enveloped and swept us into a world totally out of our control. Yet the Presence of God was around us. My thoughts and emotions were rushing and whirling within me. How could things have changed so rapidly in just a split second? Every "what if" that could possibly be suggested by the enemy of my soul bombarded me and did its best to evilly lodge in the depths of my spirit.

As we entered the emergency room, we were ushered right past the registration desks and into a room where the chief doctor met us. He began to carefully examine the cut and then clipped out some orders to his aides to notify x-ray he was on his way down with his little patient.

Stephen and I tried to sit and be calm while we awaited the x-ray report, but it was just too much to ask. We both paced back and forth, back and forth, trying to reassure each other our baby girl was going to be just fine.

Finally, the doctor came back shaking his head. He couldn't understand it. There was not one sign of concussion, not even a hairline fracture could be found. We both began to praise the Lord right out loud, right there in the hallway of the ER. He looked at us a little strange, but I suppose he had probably seen a lot of strange things working where he worked.

Next we were told that she needed a lot of stitches. I immediately made a request that a plastic surgeon be called in to do the needed work. It just so happened that two were in the hospital. They explained to us that that was most unusual. Usually they had to be called in.

Both doctors came quickly to the ER. A room was set up for them with their needed tools. The doctors explained that they really didn't want to put Jordan out. I kept thinking to myself, "She's just a baby, Lord. Make this easy on her, please." This didn't sound so easy.

~

I KEPT THINKING TO MYSELF, "SHE'S JUST A BABY, LORD. MAKE THIS EASY ON HER, PLEASE."

~

They allowed me to sit on the hospital bed beside her with Jordan lying down flat on her back, with her face draped. They numbed the forehead area and gently talked to her explaining to her on her level of understanding, what they were going to do. I quietly sat by her and rubbed her legs while her Dad (also standing right beside her) and I both reassured her everything was going to be fine.

I prayed out loud asking the Holy Spirit to guide the plastic surgeons' hands and to help Jordan relax and not move. You could literally feel the Holy Spirit enter that room. I believe the doctors could too. One of the doctors looked up and quietly said, "She's asleep." We all couldn't believe it, yet it was true. God had put her to sleep while they worked on her.

When the doctors were through, they explained to us that Jordan had needed over fifty stitches in her little forehead. We were given antibiotics and a cream to put on the stitches. Then an appointment was made for a follow up visit at their office within a few days. They both also inquired about where the church was and asked if it would be alright to come and visit. We both assured them we would love that. God works in mysterious ways His wonders to perform.

~

ONE OF THE DOCTORS LOOKED UP AND QUIETLY SAID, "SHE'S ASLEEP." WE ALL COULDN'T BELIEVE IT, YET IT WAS TRUE. GOD HAD PUT HER TO SLEEP WHILE THEY WORKED ON HER.

~

Stephen gently carried Jordan out to the car. We stopped to get the prescriptions filled at our drug store. I remember standing waiting for this script to be filled and silently weeping, tears running down my cheeks asking God right there in the store, "When will enough be enough? We've served You faithfully and have followed You even in the hardest of times. I don't understand why this has happened, but I want You to know..."(by now I am sobbing softly in an aisle by myself), "Devil, you listen to this, too, because I want you to know also, Lord, I'm going to keep right on trusting You and serving You with everything that is in me. Thank You for Your protection over Jordan. I know you kept her. Help her to recover quickly."

I wiped my face, went and got the medicine and we journeyed on home. Jordan slept on a little cot in our room for the next few nights. The first night I heard someone moving in our bedroom and awoke to see Stephen kneeling beside Jordie's sleeping form, his head bowed in prayer. I knew he, too, was settling personal issues with God in his heart. This had been another hard testing.

Somehow I knew deep in my heart, God was pleased with our response. I believe we had passed the test.

~ PERSONAL REFLECTIONS ~

From personal experience, I have learned that there are seasons when it seems that all hell has broken loose. It will not be just one thing that goes wrong, but one thing right after another and not necessarily easy challenges. True Christianity is seen only under intense pressure. It's easy to sing in the sun, but let the storm clouds arise over us, it becomes another thing. The purity of the New Testament church was kept by the fire that raged against her. Are we in less need of purifying?

THOUGHTS TO PONDER

♦ When God begins to touch our flesh does it seem the heat of trial has been driven up by notches?

♦ Compare the prayer in the drugstore to Job's prayer when he was tempted to curse God and die.

♦ I Peter 1:7 says, "So that (the genuineness) of your faith may be tested, (your faith) which is infinitely more precious than the perishable gold which is tested and purified by fire. (This proving of your faith is intended) to redound to (your praise and glory and honor when Jesus Christ (the Messiah, the Anointed One) is revealed." Does every Christian's faith need to be tested to this depth? Why or why not?

TWENTY-TWO

~

GRIEVING THE
HOLY SPIRIT

We all began to truly focus ourselves on two main goals now that we no longer would have to fight in the legal arena. The first one was to get in the building and begin functioning as a normal church again. The second was to get our lawyers' bills paid off. Both looked like tremendously looming giants to us from where we stood.

We continued on with our prayer meetings and speaking faith and hope to one another. We had come this far. We had seen the Hand of God over and over working tremendous victories for us. We believed with everything that was in us we would be able to go in and conquer the land, the Canaan land that was ours.

We continued to meet at the motel on Sunday afternoons and as many evenings as people could come, we worked on the front part of our building. There wasn't much money to go around to buy building materials but it just so worked (actually God's divine provision), that whatever we needed next to finish a room or project, would be found in the building or the money would come just at the right time for the project to continue to move forward. You see, Deacon during this whole process of lawsuits, had had some of his men back a huge truck up to the doors of the church and empty it of as many building supplies as they could carry and fit on the truck. We were left with very little to work with. These were materials already paid for or later charged to our account that Deacon said we owed him.

A special fund was set up to raise money to pay off the astronomical lawyers' fees. We had really needed their help at the time and were thankful for it, but now it was time for us to pay the piper. We set up monthly payments and worked away at this huge mountain.

Finally we came to the place where we gratefully finished the front part of the building. Our lobby was large enough to seat around two hundred people. We urgently needed the permission from the head building inspector to start holding services there with the rest of the building not completed and then we would be good to go.

As a congregation, we began to fast and pray asking God to give us favor with this head man. To call this a major hurdle for us would be an understatement. This man was known for being tough with his inspections and a real stickler to the codes. This was a big chasm for us to cross to get back to normalcy as a church. If he wouldn't approve us, we would have to continue on worshipping one service a Sunday in the motel and no midweek activities other than what could be done in people's homes. We also would have to raise another fifty to sixty thousand dollars to get our main sanctuary done.

Stephen and Carl set up the dubious appointment to go and discuss the possibility of occupying just the front part of the building with the head inspector. They were extremely nervous, needless to say. I am so glad to report that this man was very open to us as a church and the favor of God fell upon us. We were given our CO (certificate of occupancy) upon the condition that we board off the main sanctuary while we continued to work on it. He even approved our school to reopen in the finished front classrooms.

Ecstatically, Stephen and Carl came walking out of the town building. Carl told me later that Stephen was leaping down over steps going out, two and three at a time! Oh, how good God was to us! What a major victory and black eye to the devil!

~

CARL TOLD ME LATER THAT STEPHEN WAS LEAPING DOWN OVER STEPS GOING OUT, TWO AND THREE AT A TIME!

~

What a breathtaking day it was when we had our first service! What rejoicing and high celebration, praising the goodness of the Lord in the land of the living! We could stay as late as we wanted and also we could kick in to our Sunday night service mode again. Sunday School was set back in order and our midweek and family night were recharged and fired up.

Through all of this rejoicing though, there still seemed to be something wrong that I was witnessing in my spirit, a "check" so to speak. God was not pleased about something. I began to seek Him and wait on Him for what it was.

One day while Stephen was preaching, I had my Bible opened to his text. My heart was still heavy concerning this check. "What is it, Lord?" As he was preaching, I glanced down to the open pages of my Bible lying on my lap, and my eyes were drawn to these verses, Proverbs 24:17-19. It reads, "Rejoice not when your enemy falls, and let not your heart be glad when he stumbles or is overthrown. Lest the Lord see it and it be evil in His eyes and displease Him; and He turn away His wrath from him (to expend it upon you, the worse offender)."

There it was. This was what was grieving the Holy Spirit of God! We, as a body of people had so nurtured a dislike for those who had hurt and wounded us, (and probably that is too mild of a word to actually truly describe our hearts at the time), that we had begun to grieve the heart of God. I was in shock! How could we have allowed such nastiness to come into our spirits? But there it was!

For example, if the toilets happened to back up, we would blame Deacon. We just knew he had sent someone in to plug them. Or, if we couldn't find a certain building material that had been there just yesterday, Deacon had probably sent someone to break in and take it. We really knew better. But, we had tipped over into ridiculous, bitter thinking. I bet the enemy of our souls was having a real good laugh at us. What depth of spirituality!

~
WE REALLY KNEW BETTER. BUT, WE HAD TIPPED OVER INTO RIDICULOUS, BITTER THINKING.
~

Not only were we blaming Deacon all the time for everything, at the same time, many of us were hoping and even praying that something tragic would happen to him. We became like the "Sons of Thunder" who wanted God to bring down fire from heaven and consume their enemies. We were pathetic, yet acting just like the real flesh we were.

Now God was revealing to me our (myself included), sins. What was I to do about it? I knew to confront people in their frame of mind at the time, would be like walking into a den of hungry lions; so, I began to earnestly pray.

I felt God leading me to begin by talking to the Church Board. This was not a pleasant thing to have to do. I sought God for His supernatural wisdom and covering.

I quietly and carefully began to lay out what was in my spirit one night at a monthly board meeting. You could have heard a pin drop and you actually could physically feel the anger emanating from defensive members who at great cost had stayed the course of battle to walk beside their pastors. Many had paid a very high price. And now to be told that they must search their own hearts and honestly repent and forgive and pray for the very one who had wounded them so deeply, seemed like being asked to do too much. But, after much discussion and a heavy blanket of the convicting power of the Holy Spirit falling upon us, we collectively and separately asked for forgiveness and cleansing from our poisoned attitudes and wrong negative words. The conclusion we came to: Deacon was God's business, not ours.

Next, was to present this word of the Lord from these verses in Proverbs to the whole congregation. I was up to speak the next Sunday, and quite frankly was extremely nervous about it. I knew God wanted me to explain what He was feeling in His heart.

I slowly began to explain these verses, choosing my words carefully. I knew there were multiple open wounds still festering and bleeding among us from deep hurts, betrayal among friends, emotional cuts and slashes, harmful words remembered and rehearsed day after day that would take a long time to heal. I was on sore, tender ground here, yet I knew in my heart, God would not allow us to go any further in our growth until we had dealt with our own hearts.

~

THE CONCLUSION WE CAME TO: DEACON WAS GOD'S BUSINESS, NOT OURS.

~

After fully explaining what I felt was the heart of God in this matter, I asked if we could just silently sit before God in His Presence. Oh, how God came! It was so quiet; His Presence came like a holy hush, yet electric with His power. Soon soft weeping and muffled crying could be heard among us. I continued to sit with my eyes closed as I did not want to intrude on this intimate time for us all before the Lord.

Then I couldn't help but open my eyes as I heard people begin to fall to their knees, only to stay there for just a few moments. Within this short span of time, the entire congregation, including the senior pastors and other leadership, lay prostrate on their faces in broken repentance before the Lord. Oh, what a sound of remorse! It was heart wrenching to hear this coming from these people who had been through so much. Yet, God was teaching me that just because we had been hurt and hurt deeply over and over again, that did not justify us having a wrong, hateful spirit towards anyone, even the very enemy who had so betrayed and deeply harmed us. God wanted a right spirit and godly character towards even him. Oh, what deep, maturing lessons He was teaching us!

~

HE WANTS NO STRONGHOLDS STAYING WITHIN US, NO MATTER WHAT KIND OF EXCUSES WE THROW OUT TO HIM TO CONVINCE HIM THEY SHOULD BE ALLOWED TO STAY.

~

After a season of soul searching repentance, you could feel the loving embrace of the Father come around us like a warm blanket. It felt like a cleansing bath of Holy Ghost oil dripping down over us and in us and around us. Something had definitely broken in the heavenlies for us individually and corporately as a body.

We were to never be the same again. The healing process had truly begun. We were on our way to recovery! Thank You, Jesus!

~ PERSONAL REFLECTIONS ~

It is one thing to know Scripture in your heart and another to apply it actively and yield to the working of the Holy Spirit in one's life, yet that is the process God wanted to work in all of us. It is no different today, right now.

Whatever situation we may find ourselves in today, He is the same as He was back in the days of this intensive battle. God is very good at slowing things down maybe even to a grinding halt, to deal with our hearts and attitudes. He wants no strongholds staying within us, no matter what kind of excuses we throw out to Him to convince Him they should be allowed to stay. No one is exempt from the powerful searchlight of the Father. He sees all and will deal with all. Let Him.

THOUGHTS TO PONDER

♦ Does God hold back releasing His blessings if our hearts are not right with man and God?

♦ Discuss the word "process" in light of God purifying man's heart.

♦ "Iron sharpens iron." Is it easy to discuss heart issues with those you worship with especially if the issues are grievous to the Lord such as having aught against Deacon? Are most people at a depth of maturity to allow others to discuss such issues with them?

♦ The peace of God reigning in individual hearts and as a corporate body is a top priority. If this peace is not there, what are the repercussions?

TWENTY-THREE

MS. NEWS REPORTER

God was helping us to gain great victories and to make huge strides, but the warfare was not over. The devil had planned another horrendous attack to try and take us completely out of the fight. I only tell this to help other pastors and those in leadership positions know that they too can survive and come out still able to function after living through a Chernobyl.

One day, as I was sitting at my desk, in walked one of the sleaziest news reporters we have in this city. It has been said that she would do anything for a story.

Here she stood as bold as brass, with her cameraman getting ready to fire up his equipment to film me. I didn't know what in the world she was even there for. Then she began to shoot questions at me.

What had happened was that a few "spiritual" women from the past, who were full of demons and evil had called her and told her that we had known about an incident and had not reported it to the proper authorities. The incident had not even taken place during school or church, nor was it on the church property. And here we were as a ministry trying to start up a daycare center. These women knew that and were determined to shut us down, in the hopes we would never even get started. They were telling others,

what business did we have in doing this kind of work when
we were not responsible to have done what was right concerning this situation?

The truth was that we had followed through with
contacting the authorities and dealing with the problem as
best we could although these evil women had not known
this because we did not get up in the pulpit and announce
it to everyone. Ms. News Reporter, wanting a dicey story,
would stop at nothing to try and dig up some dirt even if it
wasn't there.

I walked her out the door after telling her cameraman
to turn off his camera. I wasn't unkind, but I did not vol-
unteer any information that was not any of hers or anyone
else's business. They left.

I immediately knew I had to get my kids out of there
and get to my husband as fast as I could. I knew Ms. News
Reporter wouldn't stop hunting us down until she had found
something to go forward on. I called home and told who-
ever was there to go to our closest neighbor. They immediately went.

I then drove home. As I approached our house, sure
enough, there was Ms. News Reporter sitting in our driveway in front of our house, waiting to hector and torment
me or hopefully my husband some more.

I went to another neighbor's home, got to a phone
and encouraged Stephen to call our lawyer to contact the
news station and tell her to get off our property. He did.
She left but that was not to be the end of her.

We, as a church, now used to spiritual warfare, knew
what to do...kick into warfare intercession. We began to
seriously take authority over the enemy. This isn't always
a quickly done thing. He is the prince of the power of the
air.

Ms. News Reporter showed her segment of these
women shooting off their mouths and making false accu-

sations against us that night on the news. Then of course, unknown to me, the cameraman had kept running his camera. Thank God I had not been nasty to her, but only polite and kind. God had been with me!

The clip only ran once for a 30 second piece. Then apparently, it wasn't newsworthy enough and was dropped by the station.

Social Services was to inform us later, that this one particular "godly" woman had called them many times before, stirring up trouble and false accusations about others, only for them to find out these accusations were not founded.

This was not an easy thing to walk through. I remember upon word that it was running on the news, of falling to my face on my office floor and wailing out to God for help to just breathe and survive. Several of the church women just knelt down beside me and wept in intercession that God would arise and scatter our enemies. Thank God, He did.

~

MY FRIEND, BE AS WISE AS A SERPENT, YET AS GENTLE AS A DOVE—ONLY BE NINETY PERCENT SERPENT AND TEN PERCENT DOVE WHEN IT COMES TO THE TRICKS AND ATTACKS OF OUR ADVERSARY AND THOSE HE WORKS THROUGH. NEVER, I REPEAT, NEVER LET YOUR GUARD COMPLETELY DOWN.

~

Yet I felt like I was going to die. It's like someone took a bag of feathers and threw them out during a wind storm. Then you were told to go and gather them all up again. It would be impossible. And so it seemed it would be to me concerning the reputation of the church and us personally.

God has been good. Nothing came of it. People, in and out of the church, never mentioned it or made a big deal of it. I guess they knew the source of the dirt or else

God deafened and blinded people to the attack of the enemy upon us.

My friend, be as wise as a serpent, yet as gentle as a dove—only be ninety percent serpent and ten percent dove when it comes to the tricks and attacks of our adversary and those he works through. Never, I repeat, never let your guard completely down.

~ PERSONAL REFLECTIONS ~

It is an overwhelming feeling to be blindsided. Oh, how good the enemy of our souls is at doing just that. I speak for myself in the knowledge that if I did not keep on my face before God, especially during seasons of hard testing, I would not come through it, passing the test in victory. My prayer life and His Word are the two keeping stays. Under such attack, the Word of God that has been put into one's spirit comes back very much alive and vibrant. The Presence of our sustaining God envelops and surrounds us as only He can. It's like trying to play in a full force football game when you've only eaten a handful of cheese puffs in the past twenty-four hours; it just doesn't suffice. You would need to eat something hardy and of sustenance plus be in physical top notch condition to get in, play, take the punches and falls and still get up and be a player in the game. So is it in spiritual warfare. We must stay spiritually strong and healthy at all times feeding on the Word of God and staying in the Presence of the King.

THOUGHTS TO PONDER

♦ Do reporters have a right to barge into someone's office with cameras rolling without permission?

♦ What would your reaction have been?

♦ What should the reaction be towards these women who were slandering?

♦ Discuss the statement, "Be as wise as a serpent, yet as gentle as a dove—only be ninety percent serpent and ten percent dove when it comes to the tricks and attacks of our adversary and those he works through."

TWENTY-FOUR

RECONCILIATION ATTEMPT

God also forewarns and prepares us. The Lord gave another dream during this season of challenge. I dreamt that I heard crying coming from our conference room. It sounded like very sorrowful weeping.

As I was waking up from the dream, I felt the Lord impressing me to go to the church and anoint the conference room with oil. I felt like this was going to be an act of preparation for what was going to come.

I asked my husband and Carl to come with me. We went in together and I explained to them what I believed the Lord had asked me to do. You know how it is when God asks something of you and no one else has the same sense or mandate from God that you feel. They both just quietly sat there with their heads bowed praying.

I got up and began to anoint the dark wood panels of the walls of the conference room. As I began to pray, I felt such a sense of sorrow. I started to weep heavily yet I kept moving slowly, praying in my prayer language. The Presence of the Lord came over us like a thick, warm mantle.

Then as I finished making a full circle of anointing this room, I heard the still small Voice of the Lord say, "Now go back around again and anoint it with your tears." I just confess, I thought that these two brothers would know now that I truly had become a full fledged loony, yet I knew God wanted me to do this.

I quietly kept praying, moving around the room, anointing right beside the oil mark a drop of my tears. After making a full circle once again around the room, I felt released that I had done what God had wanted me to do. We collectively finished praying and left the conference room each to go about the business of our day.

~

"NOW GO BACK AROUND AGAIN AND ANOINT IT WITH YOUR TEARS."

~

Three days later, we received a call from a pastor friend who had been trying to mediate reconciliation and restoration between Deacon and the church. He had called to inform us that Deacon had just called him and asked if he would set up a meeting with us for him so that we could all sit down and talk. It was agreed upon that we would meet at the church in the conference room. Oh, the marvels of the Lord in His foreknowledge!

We agreed upon a date and asked some of our advisory board to be present at the meeting. Deacon also was bringing a pastor friend with him.

When the day came for the meeting to take place, just as Stephen was leaving the house to come, he received a phone call from the IRS. They were asking him delicate questions concerning Deacon and his business transactions. The implication was that Stephen possibly would have to go to their headquarters and give testimony.

In the meanwhile, the meeting was scheduled for two o'clock. It was now ten minutes to two and everyone else was arriving, yet no Stephen. Thank God one of our advisory was there with me when Deacon arrived.

It was a nerve wracking time for me. I had not seen this man since the night of horrors several years previously and now here I was to see him again face to face, and without my husband there.

In Deacon walked. We all then proceeded to the conference room and waited a few minutes for Stephen to arrive. It was not a comfortable situation. Some tried to make light conversation to help put everyone at ease. It didn't work. Finally, he arrived.

One of the pastors opened in prayer and then the discussion began. For the most part, we, along with every pastor on the face of the earth, (as far as Deacon was concerned) were dog meat, and he definitely let us all know it. He perceived he was the victim in every way. Yet he did confess after one of the pastors drew his attention to the fact that some had really been praying for him, that he had had a dream where he had seen me lying on my face in prayer for him. He quietly muttered, "I do know that Meredith has been praying for me alot."

We entered into fervent prayer again and this time the very sorrowful moaning and weeping I had heard in my dream was now being heard literally. God in His great mercy and foresight had prepared our hearts for the fact that this man was not going to be willing to work a real reconciliation and restoration.

~

WE WERE WILLING TO HUMBLE OURSELVES AGAIN AND AGAIN IF FULL RESTORATION COULD ONLY COME.

~

Oh, yes, he would work it to a point, only to the place where it would benefit him, but never on the level that God would want it to come to. He even demanded that we put an apology in the paper saying that we knew his wife was above reproach and that we never thought she had done anything wrong. We agreed to this because on her own, she never would have done anything questionable.

We were willing to humble ourselves again and again if full restoration could only come.

As we were breaking up to go our separate ways, Deacon ever so quietly pulled Stephen aside asking to speak to him privately. When they were alone, he rapidly got to his point. He told Stephen the IRS was investigating him and he was boldly asking Stephen not to testify and give them any more information.

How weird can it get that the very same day and the very same hour that we were to meet with Deacon, the IRS had called. I believe the Lord was greatly testing my husband to see if he would try to seek revenge in his own strength and manmade way or to see if Stephen had totally surrendered this man and all the hurts he had caused in so many, truly over to the Lord. Thank God, Stephen passed the test.

You see, it is not our business how to deal with another person in the many issues of life. **We are not God.** Only He sees all the details and only He knows the end from the beginning. In order for us to personally be free, we must let go of others who have wounded and tried to destroy us. This is easier said than done, but it is possible.

When God deals with someone, then you and others cannot say "so and so" did this to this one, but that it is the hand of God dealing with them, not man's hand.

Some time after this meeting, I was to go and pick Stephen and Judah up at a trucking company. Stephen was doing extra odd jobs to help earn the income we needed to survive. I knew I had to be there at a certain time to meet them. I had a few hours, so I thought I would spend some time in prayer.

As I lay on the bed, I felt a tremendous heaviness come over me. Without any understanding of why this sense of weightiness had come, all I could do was pray in my prayer language. I randomly opened my worn Bible to

the story of King Hezekiah and how he had been sur-
rounded by evil Sennacherib and his formidable army in
Isaiah 37. It looked like there was no hope for King
Hezekiah and his desperately threatened people. The story
goes on to say that Hezekiah even scraped the gold orna-
mentation off the sacred doors of the temple to try and
raise enough pay-off as a tribute to Sennacherib. Hezekiah
was extremely distressed.

He received this poignant, threatening letter from in-
sane Sennacherib. Hezekiah wisely decided to take the letter
into his prayer closet and laid it out before the Lord. The
Lord then sent a word from Isaiah the prophet for King
Hezekiah not to fear. God Himself was going to deal with
Sennacherib, the king of Assyria.

True to the prophecy, Sennacherib's army was wiped
out and then later he was killed by one of his own sons as
he stood in his heathen temple worshipping his heathen
god.

As I read this, I understood what God was trying to
tell me. Deacon was not going to make things right. He
didn't want to. It wasn't in his heart. I was so disappointed.
I cried and cried uncontrollably. I couldn't believe that we
had interceded for all these trying years believing God for
a healing and great restoration only for God to say now
that Deacon was not going to yield to the dealing of the
Lord in his life.

I felt so weak in my physical body. I felt sick to my
stomach. I knew I soon had to go pick Stephen and Judah
up. I randomly changed my clothes still feeling like I had
been hit by a fast moving train.

As I was driving past a park on the way to where I
was to meet Stephen, I heard someone pull up behind me
determinedly honking their horn. I hastily pulled over wondering what was wrong. It was the pastor friend who had
been trying so hard to mediate a work of restoration.

He got out of his car and came to my window, explaining that he had just left from having lunch with Deacon. He was sorry to tell me that Deacon's countenance was harder than ever. There would be no reconciliation or God-worked restoration.

I knew it was the truth as God had already begun to deal with me concerning this very thing. Now it truly was all in God's hands. We had done all we could do. I had been told in a service I had been in a few days previously, to get out of the way prophetically by someone who did not know me or my situation. In other words, God was telling me to stop my persistent intercession. The word from the Lord had been that I now was getting in the way. This heavenly knowledge was hard for me to take in and grasp as I deeply wanted things to be right on every level from the physical to the emotional to the spiritual.

~

IN OTHER WORDS, GOD WAS TELLING ME TO STOP MY PERSISTENT INTERCESSION. THE WORD FROM THE LORD HAD BEEN THAT I NOW WAS GETTING IN THE WAY.

~

It is one thing to try and make things right on the physical level where you shake hands and agree to disagree. It is another thing to allow the Holy Spirit to free you up in your emotions over hurts and injuries and yet it has to fully be a work of the Holy Spirit to truly be a completed work when it is fulfilled on the highest level – the spiritual level, where we become right with God, others and ourselves. Then we are freed up to really worship and serve Him as our heart was created to do and then follow effusively all that He would have for us. This was not going to be for everyone who had been involved. My heart was sorely heavy upon receiving this explicit revelation. "Why couldn't things have turned out differently, Lord?" was the cry of my discouraged and weary worn heart.

~ PERSONAL REFLECTIONS ~

I Samuel 16:1 says, "The Lord said to Samuel, how long will you mourn for Saul?" I believe there are God-given seasons of prayer that the Lord will call you to be positioned in a posture of intercessory prayer specifically for a certain person or situation. One cannot just walk away from this. At first, it seemed cumbersome and awkward praying for this man who had so wounded me and those souls precious to me in the Body of Christ. But as time progressed, I found that especially in the night seasons of laying before the Lord, wrapped in a blanket calling out Deacon's name, a genuine burden for him and his family had come. I knew the depth of suffering my family was walking through and it seemed we were going to have to drink each bitter drop to the very last dregs, until the cup had been emptied. Suffering is not easy to watch and suffering is not a comfortable bedfellow. In seasons such as these, it is a constant companion.

So when the Lord speaks to move out of that place of passionate prayer you have been in for several years, it is a traumatic thing to let go. Faith and fervency had come together to activate a depth in me, only produced while passing through hell. To let go of this steadying pillar of hope was harrowing. To have paid the price, to have lain between the porch and the altar, and still to see the battle not turned—it seemed the Lord was asking too much. Why? Why couldn't things have turned out differently? I, like Samuel, was being told to move on with my life. Disappointed? Yes. Downcast? Yes. But, as Samuel knew, I also knew. Jesus is Lord. I must obey Him, trust Him and follow where He leads.

THOUGHTS TO PONDER

♦ Why is it so important that God be the one to deal with people and not us? What usually happens when someone seeks vengeance on their own?

♦ Discuss seasons of intercessory prayer for a specific person or circumstance.

♦ Why is obedience better than sacrifice?

♦ Name some ways God can speak unexpected, detailed direction.

TWENTY-FIVE

~

DIVINE VISITATION

As time went by, we were to be tested in many ways. I remember one day while teaching school, a dear pastor friend stopped by to visit with us. Stephen wasn't in his office at the time so our friend searched me out.

This friend had just come from having lunch with Deacon. It was in this man's heart to see full reconciliation and he had tried over the years to build a bridge between Deacon and us.

I was teaching a high school class in our school, when a knock came on the classroom door. At a glance I recognized his face through the window. I quickly gave the students some seat work and quietly propped the door open as I walked across the hall to an empty classroom to greet him.

Our friend seemed extremely agitated and upset. Upon inquiring as to what was wrong, I was bombarded by harsh, critical words such as, "You need to talk to Stephen and immediately put this building up for sale. You've tried to do too much. Move on down the road and build a pole barn. Put this place up for sale right away."

I couldn't believe what I was hearing. My spirit sank to the depths of my feet. My heart was breaking in two over his words. I thought he had been standing with us. He was the one who had come to us in the early years and had given us Scripture about "being strong and doing it" and how God would give every needed workman to help build and finish the work of the Lord. Our friend had called and visited us faithfully; he had been someone whom we could confide in and we knew he truly prayed for us.

Now here he was, speaking the very opposite of everything he had encouraged us to do. I felt like he was physically beating me with a two by four. A physical beating would have been easier to bear than these harsh words spewing out of him.

He hastily left the building after saying all of this. Thank God it was the end of the school day. I hurriedly dismissed my students and supervised them as they boarded their buses.

I made my way with tear-filled eyes to my office where I locked myself in. I crumbled to the floor crying out to the Lord that I could bear no more. What was happening? Now even some of our closest friends were telling us to throw in the towel and give it all up. Build a pole barn! So that was to be the summation of all we had been through...build a pole barn.

I couldn't take much more. I felt my insides collapsing, totally caving in. I had nothing else left to hang on to. Shattering into a million pieces...losing a hold on my inward composure, all my world suddenly was shifting, spinning totally out of control. Blind-sided is the word that comes to mind.

This had all taken place on Friday. The weekend was long and hard. There were so many thoughts rolling around inside my head. Sunday finally came. As always, I was the worship leader, so the burden of leading God's people into

His Presence that day fell on me. There was not even one minute cell of my being that desired to praise the Lord, not one.

Yet by sheer willpower and naked faith, I began by just making the sacrifice of a soft sound from some dry, desert place deep within. Would I ever be able to sing the songs of Zion with a joyful heart again?!

As I continued to hesitatingly sing, a Voice ostensibly familiar began to speak gently in my overtired, wounded spirit. "I want you to dance before me." I couldn't believe what I was hearing! Here I was, at one of the lowest times in my life, on the verge of both a mental and physical collapse and the Lord is telling me He wants me to dance before Him.

~

HE KEPT SPEAKING THIS GENTLY, YET PERSISTENTLY INTO MY SPIRIT, "DANCE BEFORE ME..."

~

I tried to push this thought far below the surface of my spiritual recognition, yet it wouldn't leave me. I said to the Lord, "Lord, I believe this is You; but why? And besides we are singing only slow worshipful songs to You today, nothing fast and exciting. I just don't have it in me to lead the people into that kind of worship." He kept speaking this gently, yet persistently into my spirit, "Dance before me, dance before me. Do it now." "But Lord, we are in the middle of this slow worship song." "Now," was the only reply.

In our fellowship, there are times when we will praise Him in the dance. It is nothing out of control, but just heartfelt spontaneous worship of God in the dance. I felt myself sliding painfully and agonizingly from the organ bench. I turned my back away from the worshipping congregation so that as much of me as possible would not be seen by them. I felt so completely empty and hollow inside. If you could have dropped a penny on the inside of me, all you would have heard was the ping, ping, ping of it distantly hitting the walls of the dank caverns of inner being until the final thud of its landing at rock bottom where my overwrought spirit had sunk. What did it really matter? I felt myself so near the edge of the luminous precipice of no return, what would one more thing happening now change?

I began to slowly, deliberately shuffle my feet as everyone's attention had begun to focus on the reason why the organ was no longer playing. Why is it church folks always look at what you don't want them to?!

This truly was a sacrifice of obedience, maybe one of the greatest I would ever have to offer to the Lord, as I barely had physical strength left to move my feet. My spirit was so broken. Never had inner annihilation seemed so sure. I quietly continued to scrape my shoes back and forth, back and forth across the carpet, my legs and arms feeling like dead, heavy weight dangling precariously off me.

Shuffling back and forth, my arms went up as far as they could in surrender to Him. Suddenly the Holy Spirit came down over me like warm, soothing oil. It no longer was just "shuffling." I was completely encompassed by the awesome power of God. I started to double over under the pressure of the heavy Hand of the Living God.

Before I realized it, I was laying face down on the carpeted floor. I felt hot, steamy tears flowing from my eyes in an uncontrollable gush just as if a dam that had held itself together for a long time now broke loose inside me. All I could do was cry.

Then out of my mouth came laughter. "What was that?" I thought. Why was I laughing? I **really** had lost it now. Someone should probably call the psych ward. Unroll the straight jacket! Yet now here came the hot, wet tears again...uncontrollable, flowing over my already smudged face and onto the floor soaking a pool into the carpet.

What?! What was this overwhelming feeling? Laughter just burst forth from me again and persisted to flow out from the deep depths of my belly.

It felt like the Lord was turning me inside out like a pocket and then shaking my inner man with a Divine Hand. All of the taunt tension, worry, confusion and fear were being feverishly shaken out of my spirit. Then out burst the hilarious laughter again. What was happening?! This wasn't just a little, soft giggle. This was gut wrenching hilarious belly jiggling laughter! And boy, did it feel good! I felt like God right there and then, was healing my wounded, ulcerated inside that had become so sore through all of this prolonged testing and arduous trial.

I could hear His still small Voice, "See what happens when you get out of the way?! I can touch you and heal you. I know just how, when and where to do it." But this was so unexpected, but oh, so wonderful! My finite human mind just could not take it all in. This was a supernatural encounter happening. I shall never forget it as long as I live. And I shall never be the same again!

~

I COULD HEAR HIS STILL SMALL VOICE, "SEE WHAT HAPPENS WHEN YOU GET OUT OF THE WAY?!"

~

The thought began to come to me that I needed to pray for the children of the church, but I couldn't get up! I had this picture in my mind of Stephen coming to me and pulling me up from behind and bracing me, all of this coming to me as the laughter kept coming.

Within just a few minutes, sure enough, that's exactly what Stephen did. A line of all the children was formed and because I was so full of the Presence of the Lord,

Stephen would put my hand on the children's heads. One by one they began to be slain out in the same Spirit of God that had come to me as He now came down upon them.

Then the adults in the congregation slipped into the line. They didn't want to miss out on anything God was doing. I was so caught up in the Spirit of the Lord. Something had broken over me. I felt magnificent, totally released! I couldn't even open my eyes to see who was being prayed for. I began prophesying and encouraging people, not even realizing who I was speaking to. The adults began to fall over under the power of the Holy Spirit receiving into their spirits what God was speaking to them.

I was so full (probably better termed "drunk") with the Spirit of God that day, all they could do was drive me home and put me to bed. God had met me in a powerful way as only He can. He had come in just the nick of time. I know I couldn't have gone any further past that specific day. The load had just become too heavy.

I now understand "transference of spirit." Our dear friend had been with Deacon. Deacon, over lunch, had filled him right full to the top with his carnal and demonic thoughts, words, reasoning and tactics of the enemy. Under the overt pressure of this, our friend had spoken only what he had heard.

Be wise. Even the strongest of us can be used by the enemy, even as Peter tried to convince Jesus not to follow through with the perfect plan of God the Father, but to accomplish the ideas of man by using a manmade plan. None of us are unsusceptible to the attacks and wiles of the enemy.

In time to come, our friend came to us several times and asked for our forgiveness for succumbing to this attack of the enemy. Things are fine now, our friendship and fellowship is strong, yet we all learned a powerful lesson in the methods of our sly foe. He will stop had nothing to hinder and destroy the kingdom of God. The bottom line is that he wants us dead, and if that won't happen, he will do anything and work through anyone he can to get us to quit and give up the fight.

Be wise. If God has said it, it will be. Hang on, no matter what anyone else may say. God will bring it to pass. And He will not let you linger too long in the valley of despair. He remembers that we are but human. He will come to us at just the right time.

~ PERSONAL REFLECTIONS ~

To try and wait quietly upon God is to refuse to try and save one's self. That's what the three Hebrew children did. They said, "Either God saves us, or we perish in this fiery furnace. But we will not compromise in order to save ourselves." You know the story, they were thrown into the fire and that is where God met them.

The psalmist said, "The Lord will perfect (complete) that which concerns me," Psalm 138:8. God will resolve things in us and for us if we can just continue to breathe in and out until He does. Sometimes it feels like that is all you are capable of doing.

Zephaniah 3:17 says, "He will settle you down with His love." He's the initiator of this love; we are the recipients. I believe God's heart for us in times like these is that He will use the crisis to reveal His love to us, and also use it to perfect our love for Him. And to this degree that I love Him, to that degree am I freed for the rest of my life and fear no longer has room in my soul, for I have learned He is faithful to meet me in my times of crisis. At the end of my rope, He not only will help me tie a knot and hang on, but will pull me up out of the miry pit I have found myself in.

THOUGHTS TO PONDER

♦ Discuss the term "transference of spirit," human and demonic.

♦ Share a time when God met you in an unexpected way and place.

♦ Friendships can be taken for granted. Discuss presumptuous reasoning.

TWENTY-SIX

~

A THOUSAND
REALTORS

The day came, even though we had gotten enough of the building done to worship in the front part that we had to go to the congregation and tell them we did not see how we were going to survive financially. Lawyers' fees had accumulated to thousands of dollars; there was no money to continue to finish the sanctuary; the monthly mortgage payment was barely being met. After much wrestling and soul searching in prayer, Stephen and I came to the conclusion that our "Isaac" must be laid down. It seemed impossible that we had come this far only to have to throw in the towel now, but...truthfully, here we were. Reality was like a sharp, hewn, pointed knife slashing wildly at our dulled minds to wake up to the hard, cold facts. It didn't look like there was any way we were going to survive.

A specially called meeting of the congregation was scheduled. Stephen and I numbly stood before our faithful congregation and quietly explained as best we could, why their church building that they had sacrificed and worked so hard for, more importantly, the vision for a great harvest on the back door of hell, had to go on the auction block. We shared our trembling, broken hearts with these precious, sincere people trying to help them understand that the building is really not the church, that they were, and if we had to worship God in a rented tent or an open field, we would stay together and do just that. We would not give in to the insidiously, appalling strategy of the enemy. He may have us in a financial struggle for survival but he could not enchain our trusting spirits. We **would** worship and continue to trust the Lord!

We had come to an incredible question in our walk with the Lord. Which is greater, God's sovereignty or His supply? We knew that God could speak what we needed financially into existence with just one word from Him, furnishing it all in a moment, yet He chose not to meet our monetary need that way.

We were in the crushing crucible of testing yet once again. God was silently looking and quietly watching to see if we would have our focus more on what He could supply for us, or were we going to focus on the fact that He is the sovereign God of the whole universe, and knows the end from the beginning and everything in between, and most important of all was knowing Him. God so often in the Scriptures assures us that our very steps are ordered by Him, that our times are in His Almighty Hand, that He knows every thought and intent of the heart of each man. We were at the place where we had been painted into a helpless corner where the God of this vast universe was going to see where our trust truly lay and what our attitude of trembling hearts would be. People were openly weeping. You could hear sorrowful, heart wrenching sobs and someone just whispering the Name "Jesus."

After Stephen and I poured out our hearts to these dear, bleeding people, articulating as best we could the need to put the building on the market, we turned to leave the gloomy meeting. We were too sore of both mind and spirit from wrestling in prayer, to stay for the actual vote to put the building up for sale. As we left, members called out tender words of love and encouragement as best they could, reaching out to pat our hands or just simply touch us as we walked by.

To exit the building, we had to walk down a fairly long north corridor. That night, that corridor I had walked hundreds of times before, felt as long as a slippery uphill mile. It seemed like Stephen and I were walking in a slow moving motion picture. Legs and feet felt like lead, lifting one limb up and then another to make a much needed exit from this deep hollow of total despair. Finally, I could feel the longed for metal door in front of us swing back and the cold, crisp night air forcefully hit our faces. Gulping down long drinks of it like a desperate person drowning and coming up for the last time, we blindly made our way to the waiting car.

~

THAT NIGHT, THAT CORRIDOR I HAD WALKED HUNDREDS OF TIMES BEFORE FELT AS LONG AS A SLIPPERY UPHILL MILE.

~

Days later, the dreaded realtors began coming and eagerly walking through the building to give us estimates, etc. Inevitably they would find their way to the very room I happened to be in and then ask to speak with me. I could feel the hot rage well up to the top of my pounding head as waves of pent up emotion would rush over like hot splashes of boiling water tossed in my exposed face. It wasn't right! This was to be ours! God had said and God had promised!

Silence and solitude were needed where I could stridently pace for awhile and vent my anger out in prayer, (if you could call it that). This happened numerous times until one crucial day as I was trying to get past my volcanic frustration as yet another unassuming realtor came by, I heard the still small Voice of God say, "A thousand realtors can walk through this place! It doesn't change **My** plan at all! I will accomplish what I have promised!" I felt revitalization flow through me! What a relief! God was going to work something magnificent for us! I now had such a deepening assurance no matter how long it took, that God was going to move on our behalf.

~

"A THOUSAND REALTORS CAN WALK THROUGH THIS PLACE! IT DOESN'T CHANGE MY PLAN AT ALL! I WILL ACCOMPLISH WHAT I HAVE PROMISED!"

~

Within this same time period, I had felt the Lord calling be aside to spend an evening in prayer at the church. Some of the board members heard about this and decided to join me. Again it was one of those times when you are the only one sensing the leading of the Holy Spirit and others are there to be supportive but really are not on the same page with you. That evening, the scripture in Zechariah 4:9 came to life for me. It says, "The hands of Zerubbabel have laid the foundations of this house; His hands shall also finish it." This passage seemed to leap off the page right into my spirit. I knew God was telling me that He had laid the foundation of this building and that He was more than able to bring it to completion. I shared this with the board members there to agree in prayer with me, and tried to encourage them to have a restful faith that God was working even though we could not see it with our physical eyes. After spending some time and study over this verse, I shared it with the congregation that God was assuring us He would bring this building project to completion.

It seemed like a very long time that I carried this verse around in my spirit. As was said of Joseph, "the word of the Lord tried him," so it was with me. It just kept rolling around in my spirit night and day, "Zerubbabel has laid the foundations of this house; His hands will also finish it," over and over again. It was there for a very long season of time. I would wake in the night and it would be there. I would go to work and try to focus but it somehow would push its way to the center of my thinking.

One Sunday as Stephen was preaching, as usual I was trying to focus but was unable to because of this verse, "Zerubbabel has laid the foundations of this house; His hands shall finish it," when I suddenly decided I was going to stay after church and pray the afternoon over this verse to try to wrestle it to the ground and get some closure and resolution on it once and for all.

After service I asked Stephen if he would take the children home and give them lunch so that I could stay through. He agreed and I went off to my office to get down to business with the Lord. As I began, my angry frustration seemed to break loose like an overflowing dam. I picked up a book lying innocently on my desk and threw it across the room, all the while talking to nobody, "I think I'm going crazy. I know I must be going crazy!" Knowing that the willpower and focus was not there as I had wanted it to be, I decided to go get a bite to eat at some friends' home and then try to come back and pray. All I did throughout lunch was to discuss this verse of scripture. My friends were sympathetic and agreed they would continue to pray with me concerning it.

That evening we had a guest speaker come to minister to us. Clive was an old timer who knew the voice of God. He had experienced the supernatural many times in his own life. Clive was speaking out of the book of Nehemiah about Nehemiah building the wall and the thoughts concerning staying focused on building, not coming down, etc. He was acting very agitated and edgy while he was trying to deliver his message. Suddenly he stopped and began to prophesy to the congregation. He said, "I don't know what this means but the Lord keeps telling me to tell you, 'The hands of Zerubbabel have laid the foundations of this house; his hands shall also finish it." Well….the congregation jumped to their feet and began to praise the Lord in high, high praise. It was marvelous! Clive stood there looking totally bewildered. He had no idea what that verse meant to us. He continued to stand looking befuddled over something, when he called me forward and said to me, "Come closer. I don't want everyone to hear this, but the Lord would say to you, you're not going crazy!" Hallelujah!!! What a word from the Lord! Poor Clive thought I really was struggling with really losing it, like a breakdown or something. He didn't have an inkling of a clue that I had had an outburst just that afternoon before the Lord. God was speaking to me, so intimately! I love Him, He is so faithful.

Also within this time period, we had been invited to visit a conference a fellow pastor was having at his church in a neighboring city. We told him we were going to be on vacation, but would come to his closing service as we would be back that same day. The man teaching the seminar, felt to minister to some that were there. The first ones he spoke to were Stephen and me. We were dressed in vacation clothes, nothing fancy just T-shirts and jeans and looking scruffy having just returned from our vacation. We were sitting towards the back trying to look inconspicuous. He began by pointing us out and then saying, "I believe I am speaking to you two ministerially." He did not know we were pastors. There was nothing about us that would have suggested that. He prophesied a few things which got our attention concerning our ministry. Then he said, "Your days of lack and doing without are over. God is going to provide what you need." We felt it definitely was a word from the Lord and continued to pray about it.

Soon after that, we felt led by the Lord to have a

sacrificial praise service in the uncompleted sanctuary. This would be our sacrifice of praise to the Lord. The men took down the temporary doors that sectioned off the sanctuary and we all filed through into the construction site. We were so desperate for "Zerubbabel" (a type of Christ), to complete this sanctuary. Also in Zechariah 4:7 it says, "For who are you, O great mountain of human obstacles? Before Zerubbabel you shall become a plain, a mere molehill! And he shall bring forth the finishing gable stone with loud shoutings of the people, crying grace, grace to it!'"

As we all gathered in the uncompleted sanctuary, we each found something we could make a loud noise with. Many found sticks of wood or pieces of metal to clack together. The older boys found long pieces of tin and other metal to bend and make noise with. Others found pipe and other kinds of plastic tubing which they could use for a makeshift horn. One of our drummers put two construction barrels together and began to play a loud rhythm on them beating on them with sticks of wood. Even one of our oldest saints sitting in a rolling chair had two pieces of wood, banging them together to make as loud of a noise as she possibly could.

~

"YOUR DAYS OF LACK AND DOING WITHOUT ARE OVER. GOD IS GOING TO PROVIDE WHAT YOU NEED."

~

We began to pray, and then we praised and made loud cacophonous worship as unto the Lord. We were collectively offering up the sacrifice of praise and faith. If someone had walked by at just that time, I'm sure we looked like possible candidates for the funny farm. What a strange sight and peculiar sound! Then we began to shout and pray "Grace, grace, Your grace, Lord," to the four corners of our sanctuary. The Presence of the Lord came powerfully that night. It seemed as if the angels came and joined our unruly band and choir. This is a memory I shall cherish for the rest of my life. We were sacrificially praising the Lord on this side of our Jordan. I know His heart was most pleased with us that night. Proverbs 18:21 says, "Death and life are in the power of the tongue, and they who indulge in it shall eat the fruit of it (for death or life)."

Less than two weeks after being in the special service at our friend's church and receiving the word from the Lord about our days of lack and doing without being over, a valued and much loved couple in the church asked to have a meeting with Stephen and myself. We thought it was to give them counsel for some personal struggle or decision they were walking through. As we sat there, this gentle brother got kind of teary and began to explain to us what he was doing. All the while he was sliding a check for ten thousand dollars across the table to us. I had to look twice! At first I thought it read one thousand dollars, but no. It truly was ten thousand! They had come into a financial blessing and wanted to bless the church and help secure the building as well as the finishing of the sanctuary. Oh, how faithful God was to us!

Also a dear woman in the Lord, a powerful minister of music, came and gave a remarkable concert as a fundraiser for us. Over ten thousand dollars was raised that one night for us to be able to go on and complete what had been started. The Lord has His own who will rally to the help of others in the Body of Christ. Her loving kindness in standing beside us through those hard years will never be forgotten by the folks of our body.

God graciously intervened for us. First the testing, which at the time seemed to never come to an end; we had to work through the cycle of hurt, then anger, repentance, then despair, then a total laying down of our "Isaac." Only then would God pick it up and work the miracle of His provision for us. You see, He wanted to receive **all** the glory. If the provision had come through the works of our own hands, we would have said we had done this. But God brought us through His grand cycle to total desperation and absolute dependence upon Him and then to a full heart surrender to His perfect sovereignty.

~ PERSONAL REFLECTIONS ~

Hindsight causes me to question myself—why couldn't I have had more of a rest in the Lord during this time? If put in a similar situation today, I would know better how to "labor into that rest" because of the past faithfulness of God that I have experienced. The question now presented to me is: am I fully trusting His timing and His ways in the challenges of this day and this particular season I now find myself in? Do I see His hand in my wilderwilderness or is that just something I read about in books about other peoples' lives? Do I recognize my wilderness dry times as actually preparation to train me to move up into the next level of all that God has for me? Have I learned that even when things look their darkest and humanly speaking, all seems hopeless, that I can still trust God is in it all? He, as His Word says, can "make a way where there seems to be no way." Glory to His Holy Name.

THOUGHTS TO PONDER

♦ Was it right that the building be put on the market? Was God looking for a total surrender?

♦ Can a person mature to the place where "none of these things move me?"

♦ It says that Abraham staggered not at the promises of God. Would you consider this a "staggering moment" of the pastors?

TWENTY-SEVEN

DEDICATION DAY

Work began again on the sanctuary. It was like the time had come for someone to switch on a light and in our case, that someone was God. We began to receive enough financially to pay our bills as well as start up work again on the uncompleted sanctuary.

We had been worshipping in our lobby and it now was getting a little tight for us to fit everyone in. After our heartfelt repentance as individuals and collectively as a congregation, it seemed God's Presence and release had come to us in an increased measure.

We needed at least sixty thousand dollars to finish the sanctuary. We had to make every piece of building material work. Calculations had to be thought out and then rethought out and double checked for accuracy. For example, we had ordered our carpeting. By some miscalculation or just not noticing, we had not ordered enough for the vertical front of the altar. It seemed like such a crisis at the time because there was just not enough money for mistakes. Then one of the men came up with a really creative idea to put beautiful wood in that area that matched perfectly with the rest of the wood in the building. We began to notice God had a better way of doing things over and over again to make His house look its best. We began to trust Him even more over every detail of His plan.

What joy there was among us now!! You could hear people singing and praising the Lord throughout the building as they came to help in whatever way they could. There are so many that gave of themselves sacrificially to help complete this job. But no one wants to be named. We want all the glory to go to the One who fully deserves it all. Without Him, we were nothing, and it still is that way around here 'til this day.

Soon the sanctuary was completed! The dedication day was set and invitations were sent out far and wide. Our new chairs were delivered, velvet curtains were hung from built-in supports. The new pulpit was carried in and set in place. Every piece of furniture, every stroke of the paint brush, every sound of a vacuum cleaner running brought awesome leaps of uncontrollable joy welling up and overflowing within us.

Finally the day came for our long awaited celebration and dedication. Remember, the devil is never happy when we step into his territory and declare it ours. That particular day of dedication, our oldest son decided it would be his day of stating his declaration of independence. He had not been living right and as teenagers will, had been rebelling against the rules and authority at home. It seems to me, that the devil is constantly looking for chinks in pastors' (and the rest of the five fold's) armor. He never relents.

~

REMEMBER, THE DEVIL IS NEVER HAPPY WHEN WE STEP INTO HIS TERRITORY AND DECLARE IT OURS.

~

As we were leaving for church, dressed in our celebration clothes, our oldest son was moving his things out of our house. This was a first for us. He was the oldest son. Our hearts which should have been exploding with overwhelming gratitude, were oozing with severe pain and worry over this son we loved so much. Why today of all days?!

Stephen and I staggered down the aisle to the new altar, knelt down together and laid our faces in the brand new carpet. We both just wept. It sounds so simple, but that's all we could do. We had no more words. What a whirlwind of emotions washed over us. Together we clung to the only solid One we knew...Christ Jesus, our Solid Rock. Somehow as we lay there, a deep peace began to permeate our spirits. We shared a box of Kleenex together, stood up and helped each other straighten out our disheveled clothes, braced ourselves and determined we would rejoice in the Lord this day no matter what the enemy tried to do to hinder us. We literally squared our shoulders, spoke His Name one more time and went on about our duties.

~

"PASTOR, THE LORD WOULD SAY TO YOU, YOU WILL NOW BUILD AN ORPHANAGE."

~

What a day of celebration! Finally...as God had said it would be. (But how many years it had taken to get to this place?) You can only imagine the high praises and joyous sharing on that day.

Our guest speaker was the former president of our Bible College. He had semi-retired several years before, but was still speaking out when asked.

I don't even remember what the theme of his message was. Stephen and I were sitting on the platform listening in contemplation and silently rehearsing all that God had accomplished when suddenly Dr. Blessing turned while still preaching his dedicatory message and pointed to my husband and began prophesying. He said, "Pastor, the Lord would say to you, you will now build an orphanage." Stephen was so stunned. He looked like someone had just sucker punched him very hard in the stomach! He first went white and then a pinkish red. I knew why.

Many years ago when we were in college, Stephen had had a tremendous burden to build an orphanage. He had prayed for several years about doing just that with the burden of it never fully lifting off him.

Over the years we had become busy and involved in pastoring and working in that area of ministry. We had come to the conclusion that building an orphanage had probably just been something we were emotionally moved over and maybe all our involvement would ever be, was to be a prayer support and financial givers to another's work in this area.

What a shock on this particular day, the dedication day of this long, arduous journey to complete this leg of the ministry in our lives; when we thought we could lay down the trowel and the sword for a much needed reprieve, rest and relaxation, to now receive this word, "You will now build an orphanage." What was God thinking?! How could this ever be?! We knew we had heard from God just as if He had stepped into the pulpit Himself and had breathed out this command to us directly.

As time went on, we continued to ponder this prophetic word and lift it up to the Lord in prayer. Did he mean exactly what He had said or did it have some deeper "spiritual meaning"?

One Sunday evening some time later, just as service was about to begin, in walked a pastor friend with another brother I had never seen before. As this stranger walked into the sanctuary looking for a place to sit, the Spirit of the Lord spoke strongly to me, "You and your husband are to wash this man's feet tonight in the service." I was sure I was hearing from the Lord.

I asked the ushers to please prepare a basin, towel and water for a foot washing later in the service.

At the appropriate time that evening I explained to the congregation and other leadership there that I felt God wanted Stephen and me to wash this guest brother's feet. The ushers brought out the basin, water and towel as this man came forward and sat in a chair placed in the front for him. Stephen and I both knelt down on our knees and began to each wash a foot of this dear brother. As we were washing, we began to pray and weep over him. As things progressed, our pastor friend that had brought this man to service began to explain that he was a pastor from Kenya and that he had been feeding orphan children on pennies, doing the best he could with the little he had. These children were living in little shacks and hovels with barely enough food and clothes to sustain them. As we were on our knees, it all became crystal clear the reason God was saying "wash this man's feet." God was revealing yet another step in His plan and destiny for our lives. Great rejoicing could be heard that night among us as God made His direction so apparent.

~ PERSONAL REFLECTIONS ~

I am pleased to report that this eldest son is now serving the Lord with a full heart and is a great strength to us, his parents. He has married a beautiful young woman, full of the love of God and they both are serving as leaders in the Body of Christ. You see, God knew the outcome of this son's life when all we could see was the immediate circumstance. We have come to understand that God has a specific timing for each one of us when He knows we will be ready to allow Him to work a deeper work and experience within us.

Our son could have continued to play "the game" that pastors' kids know how to play so well, just to please mom and dad. But that wouldn't have been genuine and he would have been just as far away from God sitting in the church as he would have been out doing his own thing.

Thank God, through much prayer, faith and waiting on God's timing for our son, he miraculously came back home to the Lord and to his place within the Body of Christ. To God be all the glory for His timing and His ways.

Years later, an orphanage has been built in Kenya for these children under our ministry. From the day we washed this Kenyan brother's feet, we have clothed, fed and educated these children plus many others. A beautiful facility has been built there by our people and there are mission trips coming and going from the States to Kenya all the time to reach out medically, educationally and spiritually in this needy part of the world. Oh, the plans and ways of God...they are past finding out!

THOUGHTS TO PONDER

♦ Discuss God's timing—"The time had come for someone to switch on a light, and in that case, that someone was God."

♦ Why does the enemy inevitably throw a demonic grenade in the middle of such great times of joy? Should we always try to be on the lookout for some attack to happen during or right after a high time of thanksgiving and celebration in the Lord?

♦ God allowed this attack to come to us through our eldest son at just this time. What were some of the lessons God may have been trying to teach us?

TWENTY-EIGHT

FACE THE NORTH

God is completely faithful and trustworthy. He knows exactly when to speak a word of encouragement and hope to you. There have been so many times when I felt like a weary traveler trying to make my way across a dry, arid desert without any water and the hot day's sun beating down hard on top of my weary head. At that time, it would look like from my point of view, there was absolutely no relief in sight.

It would be about then that God would send a refreshing word to rejuvenate and recharge us to go the distance. You could say He would send a soft, gentle refreshing breeze from the interior of heaven, just enough for you to sense vitalized life and sight. This was what happened to us at a very long, dry period of trying to make forward progress. Even though we had entered our Canaan land, there still was much to be conquered such as lawyers' fees, a mortgage, establishing new outreach, and continued ongoing healing for all.

Stephen and I had gone with a group from the church to a prayer conference in another city. One night while we were there, I had a dream of seeing all the folks who had walked through the fire of trial who had faithfully prayed, moving forward on their knees and were continuing forward by faith to see the church to completion, (the faithful core), all standing in the front of the completed church at the altar.

The Word of the Lord that came in the dream to them was to face the south. Then I saw the nephew of Deacon, a wonderful young man who had paid a dear price to walk with the call and vision of God, sitting down in front of us and Stephen and I washing his feet. The sense in my heart was that it was a sign to God and the heavenlies that we had done all that we could do to work restoration with Deacon's bloodline represented by his nephew who had sacrificially made the decision to follow the leading of the Lord in staying with his pastors and fellow brothers and sisters in the completion of the vision that God had given. He now serves as one of the children's pastors and does an excellent job under a powerful anointing.

I knew that this dream was from the Lord. I shared it with Stephen and the sense was that we were to literally do this.

The next Sunday we asked for those who this dream described, to come forward and we collectively faced the south. Immediately the story of Moses and the children of Israel leaving Egypt came to our minds. One of the brothers in the back of the church unexpectedly blew a shofar (ram's horn). He never had brought one to service before, but on this particular day had felt strongly to bring his.

As we were standing there, we explained that part of the dream was to wash this young man's feet as a symbol of doing all that we knew to do to work reconciliation and restoration. We felt a release that we had been obedient to the Lord in doing this, thus signifying that all had been done to try and work reconciliation and healing.

A few months after this happened, a prophet was invited to come and minister to the church. He was from Florida and had no idea of what our church had been through. He began by telling the congregation to stand and face the north and that the Lord would now take care of our enemies in the south.

Needless to say, the whole congregation rejoiced in amazement at the timing and exact clarity of the Lord! Truly He was giving us a spiritual renewing and charging to go forward and that He was pleased with our spirit. We had tried to stay as pliable and obedient to Him as we could through all of this, even though at times we felt very near death.

～

I TELL YOU THESE STORIES TO ENCOURAGE YOU NOT TO GIVE UP EVEN IN THE DARKEST TIMES OF YOUR TESTING. GOD KNOWS WHAT HE IS DOING AND WILL BRING HIS WORD OF ENCOURAGEMENT TO YOU RIGHT AT THE EXACT MOMENT YOU NEED IT.

～

I tell you these stories to encourage you not to give up even in the darkest times of your testing. God knows what He is doing and will bring His word of encouragement to you right at the exact moment you need it. It is your part to keep your spirit soft and pliable before Him. He will lead you. Psalm 37:4 says, "Delight thyself also in the Lord; and He shall give thee the desires of thine heart." Delight in the Hebrew language is **anag** meaning to be soft or pliable in God's hands allowing Him to transform you into a new spiritual creature, of course, then He can give you the desires of your heart. He's simply asking you to be spiritual clay for Him.

~ PERSONAL REFLECTIONS ~

Somehow today, the clarity of the Lord doesn't seem to be as intense as it was back then. Yes, there are moments and a few times here and there that God speaks loudly. My thought is that possibly He draws near to us in our most dire times to help carry us through them. Someone once said in my presence that they wished they had had such experiences of hearing and seeing the hand of God move in their lives. A colleague who was there spoke up and said, "Yes, wouldn't we all, but are we willing to walk through the hard times in this way in order for God to speak to us like this?" Good question. Was it a matter of being in prayer so much that drew us near to Him to hear Him clearly? What are the elements that come together to hear His Voice and understand His ways? Only pressing into Him will give us those answers.

THOUGHTS TO PONDER

♦ Is there a secret to having dreams and visions or is it as God chooses to give them to certain individuals?

♦ Have you caught a glimpse of God's infinite care for individuals as well as congregations in bringing them up-to-date on what is in His heart for them?

♦ Has there ever been a desire in you to hear God speak clearly and directly to you whether it be through a sign or dream or whatever method He would choose to communicate to you? Have you thought it was only for others?

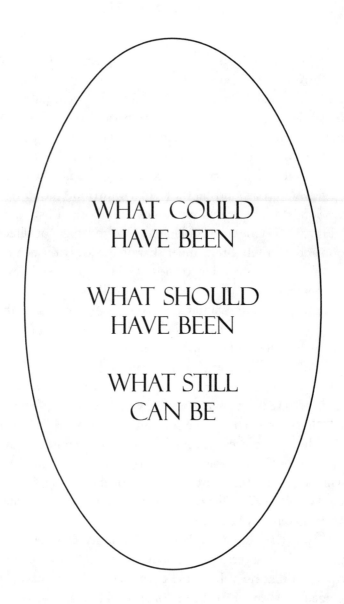

WHAT COULD
HAVE BEEN

WHAT SHOULD
HAVE BEEN

WHAT STILL
CAN BE

EPILOGUE

Looking back so many years later, my heart is still sorrowful when I ponder over all the water that has gone under the bridge since then. As I think of the past and those who chose to walk another path, I still remember the powerful times we all shared together in the Presence of the Lord, the times we lingered together around the altars, no one really wanting to leave to go home, the times of fellowship around tables loaded with food, good discussion, sharing dreams and hopes with those of like spirit and faith. I remember looking to God together for direction and counsel. I remember sharing the joys of watching people of all ages coming to know the Lord together, knowing that each of us had played a small part in that one being there; sharing family occasions like weddings, birthdays, even funerals over the years that were to bind our hearts together in healthy laughter and deep felt sorrow.

What could have come from this kind of uninterrupted communion—a greater reaping of the harvest that could have affected that many more lives; powerful effectiveness in collective mission efforts all over the world? Other churches and outreaches sent out from our church body? A rising up of dynamic young people to go into ministry whether within the church structure or the marketplace as God would lead? What could have been? Only God knows what was in His heart...

What should have been was a unity founded and grounded in prayer; a people so humble and broken before the Lord that no wile of the enemy could have pulled or tugged us away; a mature people quickly ready to cover one another's back, ready to fight wholeheartedly for their brother or sister's advancement rather than their own. What should have been for some was a coming into their own as marketplace movers and shakers affecting the world around them and beyond; teachers and trainers oozing over with anointed God-given talents teaching and training the next generation; families being trained from one generation to another how to carry on the work of the Lord. My heart is heavy in my reminiscing because there are families because of their parents' decisions, who've lost out through fleshly stubbornness, their ability to pass on Godly heritage to them, their children and their children's children. Just within my lifespan, the very next generation to mine for many is walking far from God, not even within a touching span of the circumference of the holy. Oh, how far one falls when we step out of alignment with God. How many others are no longer even attempting to walk with God with only a lingering, tender, touching remembrance of the Presence of the Lord they used to experience in days of old?

But, thank God, I am able to still think this last thought—what still can be? Doesn't God tell us He is the God that restores the years that the cankerworm and locust have eaten away? How does He do this after so much time and so many events have taken place? I don't know, but I know He can. What can be done with the rest of the time each one of us has left? Whose life can we affect? Can we still instill godliness in our children, grandchildren and those still to come after us? Can we somehow, with God's help, make a greater mark through our true, heart-felt repentance and humility before God and man than any other known act we could ever do in our lives? Only God knows. Could we still affect our dying community and needy fields afar? I believe so. The door is still open. The light is still on.

~ ALSO AVAILABLE ~

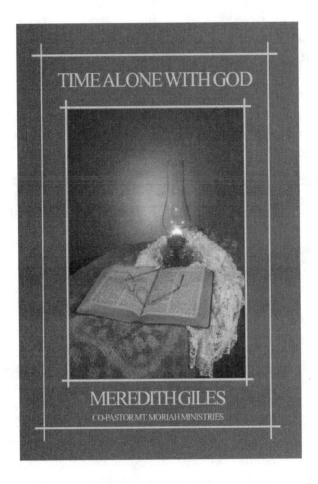

TIME ALONE WITH GOD

MEREDITH GILES
CO-PASTOR MT. MORIAH MINISTRIES

FOR INFORMATION CONTACT:

MEREDITH GILES
PO BOX 189
FEURA BUSH, NEW YORK 12067
magiles1@juno.com

~ BOOK REVIEWS ~

"In the course of our every day life, our hand reaches for the door marked 'Today', only to discover once it is opened, we may be brought face to face with heartache, challenges and an uncertain future.

Time Alone With God is birthed from the fabric of one woman's life who, through faith in God, trust in His Word and integrity in character, shares devotional thoughts and insights to encourage the weary heart."

Gail Rozell, Pastor/Co-founder
Montgomery Heights Children's Home, Zimbabwe

"This devotional drawn from the rich heritage of a Christian family contains material that's likely to change your life. The truths being read every morning at Barnabas Ministries' daily prayers have challenged and encouraged, often just on the day that we needed it most. But don't take my word for it, this is a MUST read book designed to encourage you to look beyond the ordinary to the divine."

Jeanne Wyns, Co-founder
Barnabas Ministries, Rhode Island

"I have watched Meredith's life for well over a decade. Her intimacy with our Savior has birthed the eternal truths shared in this devotional. Drawing from a rich Christian heritage, as well as personal experience, she comforts, encourages, and cajoles. You may laugh, cry, or confess on any given day and I guarantee you will grow in the grace and knowledge of our Lord Jesus Christ. Pull up a chair and enjoy."

Iris Pelley, Co-founder
Frontline Ministries, Rhode Island